Experience and Learning

An Introduction to Experiential Learning

By Arthur W. Chickering

Change Magazine Press

Change Magazine Press gratefully acknowledges permission to reprint the following:

Material on pages 13, 14, 17, 65, 81, 86 from *Experiential Learning: Rationale, Characteristics, and Assessment* used with permission of Jossey-Bass, Inc.

Material on pages 15, 16, 54, 69 from *Experience and Education* used with permission of Kappa Delta Pi, An Honor Society in Education, P.O. Box A, West Lafayette, Indiana 47906, owners of the copyright.

Material on pages 17, 18 from *Theories of Group Processes* used with permission of John Wiley & Sons, Inc.

Material on pages 54, 55 reprinted with permission of *The Journal of Applied Behavioral Science.* "The Design of Cross-Cultural Training: An Alternative to the University Model" by Roger Harrison and Richard S. Hopkins, Vol. 3, No. 4, pp. 437-438. Copyright by NTL Institute, 1967. Material on page 68 from "Two Tramps in Mud Time" from *The Poetry of Robert Frost*, edited by Edward Connery Lathem. Copyright 1936 by Robert Frost. Copyright © 1964 by Lesley Frost Ballantine. Copyright © 1969 by Holt, Rinehart and Winston. Reprinted by permission of Holt, Rinehart and Winston, Publishers.

The Change Policy Papers

1. Faculty Development in a Time of Retrenchment
2. Colleges and Money
3. The Testing and Grading of Students
4. **Experience and Learning**
5. Professional Development: A Guide to Resources
6. Competency-Based Learning

six

This report was prepared under a grant from the Danforth Foundation. Their support is gratefully acknowledged.

Acknowledgments

Most of the ideas shared in this book come from experiences with students, faculty members, and administrators who helped create Empire State College, and from colleagues who participated in the Cooperative Assessment of Experiential Learning (CAEL) Project. Early drafts were considerably improved by critical reactions and substantive suggestions from Richard J. Allen, Director of the Division of Arts and Sciences at Johns Hopkins University; Donald Casella, Director of the Contract Learning Center at Birmingham Southern College; John Duley at Michigan State University; Barbara Graves and Jon Wagner of the Field Studies Program at the University of California, Berkeley; Cyril O. Houle, Professor of Education, University of Chicago; Morris Keeton, Executive Director of CAEL; and Robert Sexton, Executive Director of the Office for Experiential Education at the University of Kentucky. I also received valuable assistance from several Empire State associates: James Feeney, William Laidlaw, Lois Lamdin, Rhoda Wald, and from Jo Chickering. In addition, the editors of *Change* helped shape the original approach, and their collaboration and encouragement proved invaluable.

—*Arthur W. Chickering*

About This Report

THERE IS SOMETHING ABOUT EXPERIENTIAL LEARNING that raises the hackles of even the most unflappable academics. The debate over the values of lifelearning has set off cognitive against affective learning theorists; pitted traditionalists against those true to the human potential movement; often divided senior faculty and younger instructors; and set academic jocks, if you will, against the hipper followers of Charles Reich and Esalen. I exaggerate, of course, but only to make a point of the emotional depth to which this debate has on occasion descended. It is almost as if booklearning and lifelearning do not spring from a common human experience; as if one must choose only one mode and repudiate the other.

A decade or two ago, one could still engage in the luxury of debating such curricular options with the purity of theoretical detachment. Experiential approaches were viewed with bemused fascination, to be tried in some flakier academic establishment, but not here. Most of us were still ruled by the time-honored definition of what it meant to be educated, to be erudite. This definition, in some earlier day, was synonymous with what one gleaned from books and college lectures, which are, for the most part, a regurgitation of still more books. Whatever students learned from outside life was charitably defined as "extracurricular." *Ex curia* was more like it.

In this and other matters, however, we have both matured and been more realistically instructed by the exigencies of these new times. Experiential learning is no longer regarded as some academic foot-and-mouth disease. It is no longer thought dangerous to a student's health, nor is it in any way the panacea its earlier messiahs proclaimed it. Experiential learning no doubt can be a delightful refuge for a student's sloth. But it can also, for a growing number, bring insight where none or little was produced through booklearning alone.

One comes then to the larger, and related, matter: We are witnessing significant shifts in our culture and in the kinds of students colleges are inheriting from the high schools. They are, for one, television's children. Much can be said about that, but it is sufficient to note that they are significantly different from their parents. We can hope that they will emerge from college as more literate human beings, more appreciative of the written and spoken word. Many are clearly not so endowed when they graduate from their high schools. Should they now by some miracle be transformed between June and September? Or should college offerings be adapted so as to engage these students in ways less dependent on traditional book-based learning? Every academic must answer this question for himself.

When *Change* decided to devote one of its faculty policy papers to this subject, we sought a view that would be thoroughly honest, even-handed, and informed by the richness of both theoretical and practical background. Arthur W. Chickering is an authority with such a perspective. He understands these issues intimately and has dealt with them more thoughtfully than most other people in America. He was recently appointed Distinguished Professor of Higher Education and Director of the Center for the Study of Higher Education at Memphis State University.

At its best, experiential learning adds innumerable prisms to our capacity to learn about life and subject matter. In a modern society increasingly oriented to nonproduction careers, this habit of certifying human service competence by booklearning alone can become dangerous social nonsense. It must be evident to anyone who has ever been exposed to a doctor, lawyer, paraprofessional, social worker, or employment counselor that knowing the "material" is not enough. We need to provide better and more diverse educational opportunities so that students can have ample experiential foretastes of life to come. A greater emphasis on experiential learning will also, I hope, discourage those with insufficient competence along a wide spectrum of abilities and sensitivities. It may also reduce the boredom and irrelevance that characterize some of our undergraduate experience.

A grant from the Danforth Foundation has made this policy paper possible. The books in this series are widely read by American faculty, and both Danforth and Educational Change consider them an eminently worthwhile social investment.

George W. Bonham
June 1977

Experience and Learning: An Introduction to Experiential Learning

1
Roots and Definitions

Today's "experiential learning" rests on long and worthy traditions. But the university's emphasis on analytic, reflective, and theoretical studies and its neglect of concrete experiences, practical applications, and active experimentation have been equally long standing. The learning cycle of concrete experience, observation and reflection, abstract conceptualization, active experimentation and application holds promise for improving the substance and quality of higher education. Page 12.

2
Examples, Observations, Applications

Four courses and six contracts illustrate different levels of experiential learning. Coleman's steps in experiential learning and Kolb's conceptual framework provide a basis for examining strengths and weaknesses, problems and potentials. An Experiential Learning Analyzer suggests questions for planning a course or contract. Page 19.

3
Problems: Purposes, Substance, and Quality

Experiential learning raises questions about educational goals and student purposes. Providing adequate resources and evaluation challenges faculty competence when operating at a distance and relying on field supervisors and others. Traditional criteria for awarding credit often do not work well. Pressures for individualization and needs for additional resources can create problems of staffing, budget, institutional organization, and community relations. Page 42.

4
Problems: Institutional Support

If significant numbers of faculty and students make use of experiential learning, then broader institutional planning and coordination are required. Professional leadership and support staff must be supplied. Active support from top administrators and from the faculty will be necessary. Developing new approaches and learning to use new resources is hard work. Helping interested faculty members develop necessary competence and experience and sharing those with others may be more effective than confronting institutional policies and politics. Page 51.

5
Potentials for Students and Educational Effectiveness

The quality and usefulness of learning improve when concrete experiences and active experimentation are integrated with observation, reflection, and abstract conceptualization. Experiential learning makes possible more effective integration of professional/vocational training with liberal and general education. But specialized doctoral studies and research lead to limited faculty preparation for such efforts. When the demands of experiential settings are examined, they provide guidelines for decisions concerning sequence, emphasis, and timing, as well as for problems concerning substance and standards. Page 61.

6
Potentials for Faculty and Institutions

One payoff for faculty members is the opportunity to test theories in practice and to refine concepts, principles, and hypotheses through continuous feedback. Relationships with students become more collegial, and outcomes become more apparent. The institution develops a broader base of understanding and support through working relationships with diverse agencies and organizations. In addition, alternatives for experiential learning can expand the range of students served. Page 71.

7
Costs

Experiential learning alternatives that serve new constituencies may provide increased income that offsets added costs. The dollars necessary for added staff, space, equipment, supplies, and travel are easy to determine and control, but the costs or savings in other areas likely to be influenced by experiential learning are more difficult to estimate. Case studies are needed to document what happens in these areas. Page 75.

8
Policy Implications

Arrangements for veterans' benefits and financial aid for part-time students must change. A national network of brokering and evaluation services is needed to help students find and combine effective alternatives. Definitions of legitimate college study expressed through the codes of the Higher Education General Information Survey and state departments of education need to be revised to recognize new areas of learning. Regional differences in accrediting standards and practices applied to experiential learning and nontraditional institutions need to be ameliorated. Page 80.

Suggested Readings..88

1

Roots and Definitions

"A BURNED CHILD DREADS THE FIRE." "PRACTICE MAKES PER-
fect." "Experience is the best teacher."

Postsecondary education is rediscovering these basic proverbs.
Today's academies bear little resemblance to that grove near
Athens where Plato gathered his followers. From that early beginning, "academic" has come to mean "theoretical and not expected
to produce a practical result." Now the social role of higher education calls for more than simply academic contributions. Literary and
classical studies are still necessary, but they are no longer sufficient. Scholastic traditions and disciplinary conventions—grown
gross with the weight of new knowledge and methods, cracking, di-
viding, redividing, and recombining—no longer provide a comprehensive logic for curricula and higher learning. Pressures for tech-
nical and professional training run head-on into complex social
problems that call for a more knowledgeable, sophisticated, and
complex citizenry. Financial exigencies sharpen questions of purpose, effectiveness, and accountability. Under these conditions,
more interest in "experiential learning" is logical and imperative.

It would be premature to say that experiential learning has finally
come of age. Despite progress in some institutions and in some areas
of professional and general education, it is still far from being a mature art or science. Understanding and practice are highly variable
among institutions and programs across the country. For the most
part experiential learning is still primitive. But interest in it is now
strong and widespread and is not likely to diminish.

In large measure, the problems of experiential learning are simply those of good teaching. There are complex questions concerning
purposes, substance, and quality; concerning students' abilities and
differences; concerning the contribution and sequence of various
learning activities; concerning evaluation and certification.

For better or worse, we have made our peace with these questions when we teach familiar subject matter in accustomed modes. Any major change upsets that delicate blend of sound judgment, expedient rationalization, and self-deception. Just as a carefully layered cocktail can become a muddy mix when the bartender stumbles, so can the aesthetic qualities of education vanish and its taste appeal diminish. We then have to start over. To make matters worse, we are not sure which ingredients go together best, in what proportions, or in what order.

The purpose of this *Change* policy paper is neither to bury nor to exalt efforts at more effective integration of experience and learning. But a balanced assessment is in order. It is our aim simply to share current thinking about problems and potentials and to offer some concrete information that may help academics move toward improved education. There is no single ideal model for teaching and learning, no magic mix applicable to diverse students, purposes, and institutions. But there are many chances to miss even a reasonably sound approach. A better understanding of some general principles, practical guidelines, and basic problems may be timely for a wide range of persons concerned with higher education.

To this end we shall try to identify the major problems concerning educational purposes and academic quality, the kinds of challenges presented to faculty members accustomed to traditional practices, and the varieties of institutional resistance that can be anticipated. The potentials for more effective student learning, for faculty satisfaction, and for institutional support and enrichment are also outlined. Each teacher will have to balance problems against potentials and see which way the scales tip. Some guidelines for estimating costs and general implications for national and local policies conclude our brief review.

Administrators contemplating program changes may find some useful considerations concerning educational quality and costs in this discussion. Faculty members concerned with educational policies and with improving their own teaching may find ideas worth pursuing. Students concerned with expanding the range of their learning may recognize possibilities heretofore ignored.

I should make it clear at the outset that this policy paper concerns only what has been called "sponsored" or "guided" experiential learning: that is, learning that occurs while a student is enrolled as a part of the ongoing educational program of a college or university. I do not claim to tackle the complex problems and practices associated with evaluating and granting credit for "prior experiential learning"—that is, for "life experience" learning that has occurred before enrollment and may be recognized as fulfilling all or part of the requirements for certain kinds of degrees or programs. There is currently keen interest in this latter cluster of concerns, and relevant work is accumulating rapidly.[1] This brief volume does not attempt to reach that far, despite the kinship between the two topics.

There is nothing really new or startling about "experiential learning," about the integral relationships between experience and

---

1. See, for example, Morris Keeton, ed., *Experiential Learning: Rationale, Characteristics, and Assessment* (San Francisco: Jossey-Bass, 1976), and other publications emerging from the Consortium for the Assessment of Experiential Learning (CAEL) and from the recent offshoot of that effort, the Council for the Advancement of Experiential Learning.

knowledge. When the Bible first reported that Abraham knew Sarah, full-fleshed experience was the medium rather than lectures, print, or tape. For Socrates, the unexamined life was not worth living, and Sophocles observed that "one must learn by doing the thing: For though you think you know it you have no certainty until you try." Webster's dictionary gives "know" as the first synonym for "experience."

In his delightful and scholarly chapter on the deep traditions of experiential learning, Cyril Houle reminds us of the craft guilds and apprenticeship systems that provided so much advanced training from the medieval period through the industrial revolution. (Significantly, the original word for guild was *universitas*.) But parallel to this system there developed a guild of scholars who appropriated the term while developing institutional homes for themselves at Bologna and Paris. These models, which gradually spread both west and east, basically asked students to master content delivered by books and lectures. Even in professional areas such as medicine, learning occurred according to rules laid down by authorities. Systematic observation, dissection, and practice had no place. Thus the tradition of experiential learning has been accompanied by a deep division between "experience" and "learning" that was created by the universities and maintained in full strength for 700 years.

While vocational training was provided by the guilds and apprentice relationships, and scholarly training by the universities, the education of the elite was carried forth by the chivalric traditions. This system was highly experiential and competency based. Houle describes some of the required proficiencies:

> The squire must be able to: "Spring upon a horse while fully armed; to exercise himself in running; to strike for a length of time with the axe or club; to dance and do somersaults entirely armed except for his helmet; to mount on horseback behind one of his comrades, by barely laying his hands on his sleeve; to raise himself betwixt two partition walls to any height...to mount a ladder...upon the reverse or under side, solely by the aid of his hands...to throw the javelin; and to pitch the bar.

Moreover, these practical skills were accompanied by requirements exemplified by Chaucer's squire in *Canterbury Tales*:

> He could make songs and poems and recite,
> Knew how to joust, to dance, to draw, to write.
> He loved so hotly that when dawn grew pale
> He'd slept as little as a nightingale.
> Courteous he was, and humble, willing, able;
> He carved to serve his father at the table.[2]

Then as now, nonformal learning activities provided a rich background against which the more formal systems cut their figures. Libraries, monasteries, museums, churches, and courts provided resources and events. Annual rounds of feasts and festivals carried cultures and taught traditions. Wandering minstrels and storytellers, traveling salesmen, and itinerant tradesmen brought news, myths, and word of other lands. The local pub, inn, and village green provided meeting grounds to exchange common wisdom, examine current practice, and share and test new knowledge.

Then came the industrial revolution. Factories replaced crafts-

---

2. Cyril O. Houle, "Deep Traditions of Experiential Learning," in Keeton, *Experiential Learning*, pp. 23, 24.

men, unions replaced guilds, and job simplification reduced complex tasks to easily learned skills. Chivalry died. The once indivisible link between riches and royalty was broken. Feudalism and monarchy gave way to economic systems and the politics of republicanism and democracy. Increasingly, an educated citizenry with a wide range of professional and vocational skills became essential.

With the death of chivalry and the decline of the guilds, only the university survived—with its emphasis on content and authority and its rejection of direct experience and useful applications. In the absence of other alternatives, pressures mounted for a university education that was practical as well as theoretical and met the needs of new professions in agriculture, engineering, architecture, and forestry. The land-grant colleges evolved in the mid-nineteenth century, at about the time that the natural sciences were finally given curricular recognition by the classicists who dominated Oxford and Cambridge.

With the turn of the century, several major areas of professional preparation began to require direct experiences and practical applications as integral program elements. Medical schools, led by Johns Hopkins in the late 1900s, incorporated not only laboratory studies but also hospital internships; law schools included moot courts and clerkships; normal schools required practice teaching; forestry and agriculture curricula required field work.

Then came John Dewey's seminal contributions and efforts by educators to act on them. Dewey anchored his thinking in the assumption of an "organic connection between education and personal experience." Today's attempts to move toward experiential learning grapple with the same problems he addressed so profoundly. The slim, 91-page volume *Experience and Education*, written in 1938, still states the issues more sharply and succinctly than does any other document. Consider the timeliness of these words, remembering to take "progressive" in its generic sense of moving forward or advancing:

> If one attempts to formulate the philosophy of education implicit in the practices of the new education, we may, I think, discover certain common principles.... To imposition from above is opposed expression and cultivation of individuality; to external discipline is opposed free activity; to learning from texts and teachers, learning through experience; to acquisition of isolated skills and techniques by drill is opposed acquisition of them as means of attaining ends which make direct vital appeal; to preparation for a more or less remote future is opposed making the most of the opportunities of present life; to static aims and materials is opposed acquaintance with a changing world....
>
> I take it that the fundamental unity of the newer philosophy is found in the idea that there is an intimate and necessary relation between the processes of actual experience and education.... The problem for progressive education is: What is the place and meaning of subject matter and organization *within* experience? How does the subject matter function? Is there anything inherent in experience which tends toward progressive organization? A philosophy which proceeds on the basis of rejection, of sheer opposition, will neglect these questions. It will tend to suppose that because the old education was based on ready-made organization, therefore it suffices to reject the principle of organization *in toto*, instead of striving to discover what it means and how it is to be attained on the basis of experience.... When external control is rejected, the problem becomes that of finding the factors of control that are inherent within the experience.... When external authority is rejected, it does not follow that all authority should be rejected, but

> rather that there is a need to search for a more effective source of authority. Because the older education imposed the knowledge, methods, and the rules of conduct...it does not follow...that the knowledge and skill of the mature person have no directive value for the experience of the immature. On the contrary, basing education upon personal experience may mean more multiplied and more intimate contacts between the mature and the immature than ever existed in the traditional schools, and consequently more, rather than less, guidance by others. [3]

Dewey's paragraphs express fundamental propositions and identify basic problems that still hold true for experiential learning. These historical developments set the foundations for further changes that occurred as educational systems regained their poise after the demands and disequilibria of World War II. Cooperative education and varied work-study arrangements, developed at Antioch, Goddard, Berea, and a few other small private colleges, began to be recognized across the country during the 1950s and 1960s. Then came the Society for Field Experience Education. Founded in 1972 by educators, agency supervisors, and students, it seeks to serve the needs of these three constituencies through a quarterly newsletter it publishes jointly with the National Center for Public Service Internships and through annual conferences dealing with issues and practices.

The Cooperative Assessment of Experiential Learning Project began in 1973. It coordinated consortial efforts among 10 two- and four-year colleges and rapidly expanded to include an assembly that now has more than 220 institutional members. In fall 1976, the participating institutions incorporated as the Council for the Advancement of Experiential Learning with two primary purposes: "(1) to foster the development of educational programs using better mixes of experiential learning with theoretical instruction and to foster more widespread use of such programs; and (2) to sophisticate further the understanding and practice of assessment of the outcomes of experiential learning."

These developments have been accompanied by meetings among CAEL representatives and persons from a large number of other organizations with similar interests. This network of organizations suggests that interest in experiential learning is broad-based indeed, spanning a wide range of institutions and agencies concerned with higher education. This interest, together with the accelerating changes of the last decade, suggests that the deep divisions that have persisted since the time of the medieval universities may be healing.

Strictly speaking, all learning is experiential. To set some boundaries, we can begin by holding to Webster's simple definitions of learning and experience: "*Learning*—to gain in knowledge or understanding of, or skill in, by study, instruction, or experience; *Experience*—the actual living through an event or events, actual enjoyment or suffering; hence, the effect upon the judgment or feelings produced by personal and direct impressions." These definitions are broad enough to include as educational outcomes knowledge, understanding, and skills as well as judgment and feelings. They also include the educational processes of study, instruction, and experience as well as the actual living through of events. They recognize that both joy and suffering accompany experience and learning.

---

3. John Dewey, *Experience and Education*, (New York: Collier Books, 1963), pp. 19-21.

Our concern therefore is not confined to such events as encounter groups, field observations, travel, or work. Nor does it reject the value of lectures, print, films, videotapes and audiotapes, or other forms of mediated instruction or vicarious experience. There is no progress to be made by substituting one totality for another. The problem is to create that combination that is most effective for the person doing the learning and for the material to be learned.

The elements of that mix have been variously described, but despite minor wrinkles the level of general agreement is high. Disraeli, for example, said, "Experience is the child of Thought, and Thought is the child of Action. We cannot learn men from books." According to Coleman, experiential learning involves a sequence not unlike Disraeli's:

> In the first step one carries out an action...and sees the effects of that action.... Following the action and the observance of its effects, the second step is understanding these effects in a particular instance, so that if exactly the same set of circumstances reappeared, one could anticipate what would follow from the action.... The third step is understanding the general principle under which the particular instance falls.... When the general principle is understood, the last step is its application through action in a new circumstance within the range of generalization. Here the distinction from the action of the first step is only that the circumstance in which the action takes place is different, and that the actor anticipates the effect of the action. At this point, the person can be said to have completed the learning so that the experience he has undergone is useful to him in future actions. [4]

David Kolb's experiential learning model is similar to the steps Coleman describes. According to Kolb, experiential learning occurs through a four-stage cycle: "Immediate concrete experience is the basis for observation and reflection. These observations are assimilated into a 'theory' from which new implications for action can be deduced. These implications or hypotheses then serve as guides in-

The Experiential Learning Model

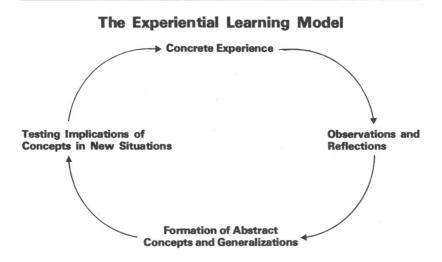

From D.A. Kolb and R. Fry, "Toward an Applied Theory of Experiential Learning," in Cary Cooper, ed., *Theories of Group Processes* (London/New York: John Wiley & Sons, 1975).

4. J.S. Coleman, "Differences Between Experiential and Classroom Learning," in Keeton, *Experiential Learning*, pp. 49-61.

teracting to create new experiences."[5] Effective learning therefore
has four ingredients that themselves call for four different abilities.
The learners must be able to enter new experiences openly and fully
without bias; they must be able to stand back from those experiences, observe them with some detachment, and reflect on their significance; they must be able to develop a logic, a theory, a conceptual framework that gives some order to the observations; and they
must be able to use those concepts to make decisions, to solve problems, to take action.

Thus the cycle involves two quite different types of direct experience: active experimentation and hypothesis testing that systemat-
ically apply general theories or propositions, and more open engagement in which such prior judgments or assumptions are sus-
pended or held in the background. It also involves two quite different cognitive processes: first, straightforward recording of reflections and observations related as closely as possible to the direct
experiences themselves, unfettered by preexisting conceptual
frameworks that might screen out or distort incongruous perceptions; and then, analyses of the interrelationships among these, followed by syntheses that suggest larger meanings and implications.

Note some critical consequences of this approach when it is
carried out well. First, experiential learning attaches major importance to *ideas*. When ideas are used as hypotheses and tested in
action, their significance and the attention given to them is greater
than when they are simply memorized or left as unexamined abstractions. An idea taken as a fixed truth gives no cause for further
thought. An idea as a working hypothesis must undergo continual
scrutiny and modification. That, in turn, creates pressures for accurate and precise formulation of the idea itself. Second, when an
idea is tested for its *consequences*, this means that results must be
acutely observed and carefully analyzed. Activity not checked by
observation and analysis may be enjoyable, but intellectually
it usually leads nowhere, neither to greater clarification nor to
new ideas and experiences. Third, reflective review requires
both *discrimination* and *synthesis* to create a record of the significant elements of the experience. As Dewey puts it, "To reflect is to
look back over what has been done so as to extract the net meanings
which are the capital stock for intelligent dealing with future experiences. It is the heart of intellectual organization and of the disciplined mind."[6] When we talk about experience and learning, we refer to this complex of interactions.

With regard to concrete examples, there is an obvious irony in
dealing with experiential learning solely through the medium of
print. We do, after all, slip so comfortably into the habitual mode so
characteristic of college and university teaching; we begin with
some introductory observations and then move quickly to abstract
concepts and generalizations. In this subject area showing is more
effective than telling, but our capacity to show is limited. Even so,
some concrete examples can illustrate the concepts, set a framework for activities by teachers, and provide a basis for later discussion of problems and potentials.

5. D. Kolb and R. Fry, "Toward an Applied Theory of Experiential Learning," in Cary Cooper, ed.,
Theories of Group Processes (London/New York: John Wiley & Sons, 1975), p. 1.
6. Dewey, *Experience and Education*, pp. 19-21.

2

Examples, Observations, Applications

I T IS SAFE TO SAY THAT BY FAR THE GREATEST USE OF DI-
rect experience to date has been in practica, internships, on-the-job
training components of professional or vocational education programs, and in the few cooperative and work-study programs currently under way. The traditional academic orientation of four-year
undergraduate institutions has meant that such programs have
been developed primarily by two-year colleges, professional
schools, proprietary institutions, and graduate schools. Indeed,
much of this paper may seem old hat to persons affiliated with such
institutions.

That reaction might be a bit premature. Practica linked to writing, readings, lectures, and examinations concerning pertinent concepts and knowledge may do a good job of professional preparation,
but they do not contribute much to the objectives and values associated with the liberal arts or general education. The professionals,
consequently, are left standing on a narrow platform as they move
on to broader responsibilities and larger aspirations. Just as those
standing in various liberal arts camps will see the mobile homes of
professional studies only dimly in the distance, so will those in the
professional and vocational camps observe the tents, tepees, and
log cabins of the liberal arts across a misty valley. There is work yet
to be done even in those arenas where experiential learning is most
naturally required and most comfortably practiced.

The social and behavioral sciences are fertile grounds for experiential learning. History, economics, sociology, anthropology, and
psychology all make use of field observations, case studies, research exercises, volunteer activities, and other activities that sup-
plement the study of texts and abstract concepts. In the human services professions supervised practice, internships, paraprofessional responsibilities, and in-service training are now a systematic
part of most programs. In these areas, effective integration of ex-

periential components with reflective and theoretical studies sometimes is a problem. Experiential opportunities often are concentrated into a single intensive period long after the pertinent theoretical studies have been completed. Frequently, the intensity of the experiential program itself precludes investing much time or energy in observation, reflection, or abstract conceptualization.

The laboratory work typically undertaken in the natural sciences aims to provide an experiential base that enriches the conceptual material at hand and helps students develop skills and techniques necessary for future original research. The cookbook exercise of the past is gradually giving way to a variety of approaches where there are real unknowns, or where contributions may be made to problems addressed by local industries or environmental organizations.

The arts have their own double-barreled relationship to experiential learning. A poem, play, novel, painting, sculpture, or symphony aims to create a direct and immediate experience for its audience. Such works link the audience to "life experience," presenting and interpreting human relationships, conditions, and events. The most powerful art seems to be that which resonates with the prior experiences and understandings of its audience. Artistic work that persists through time confronts universal dilemmas, deceits, and delusions that most people have experienced in some fashion, albeit indirectly. The lasting power and significance of good writing, with its metaphors, analogies, and rich capacity for evocation, often exceed that of film, with its explicit pictorial and aural representations, precisely because writing allows us to put more of ourselves into it.

The experience of a film or television show is almost always the experience of another person, an experience outside ourselves. We identify strongly, tears of sympathy flow, chills run up and down our spines, but its very explicitness leaves less room in which to introduce the particularities of our own past history or current circumstances. Direct and artistic experiences are inextricably linked; to be impoverished and unperceptive in the first is to have limited capacity for the second. So there probably exist unexplored and unexploited possibilities in this area. Indeed, some of the time currently invested in historical studies and critical analyses designed to increase *understanding* of art might be invested usefully in activities that help increase the ability to *experience* a work of art more directly rather than to treat it as an object for intellectual dissection, filtered through a variety of preconceived screens.

The examples that follow—four courses and six individual learning contracts—do not span the full range of disciplines and professional studies. Instead, they were selected to call attention to some of the practical and educational problems and potentials in systematic efforts to design experiential learning. They provide opportunities to apply Kolb's conceptual models. The examples are not offered as ideal cases, nor would the teachers and students responsible for them make such claims. They range from straightforward activities organized for groups of students to more complex combinations created jointly by a particular student and a particular teacher. In each case the description is followed by a few brief observations. The reader is invited to supply observations for the last three contracts.

The four courses are: Bioresearch in Environmental Studies, Race Relations in the United States, Counseling Theory and Practice, and Early Childhood Education. The six individual contracts are: Human Services and Criminal Justice, Sociology, Mental Health and Retardation Services, Agriculture and Woodworking, and travel contracts in Environmental Studies and American Studies. (These examples are from the *Contract Learning Casebook* published by the Center for Individualized Education at Empire State College.)

Bioresearch in Environmental Studies

The following course in bioresearch illustrates an approach familiar to many natural science teachers. The major objectives were "to help students gain experience and knowledge in bioassay techniques and methods as applied to environmental problems" and "to increase the ability to plan research projects, evaluate results, and write final reports." Each student will design, carry out, and report on a research project. The exact nature of the project will be worked out in consultation with the instructor, but it will involve a study of the environmental toxicity of a particular chemical, using fish as subjects. The following activities will be included:

A. Background reading and study in biology, biology of the fish, ecology, biology of water pollution, and bioassay techniques and methods (see attached bibliography). Further readings will be identified as each project becomes focused and the student will keep notes on all readings, which will become part of the bibliography for his final report.

B. A visit to the Environmental Protection Agency Bioassay Laboratory to learn more about specific techniques and methods. Each student will prepare a report on this visit.

C. Planning and writing a formal research project proposal, including background for the problem, objectives, and methods.

D. Carrying out the project and collecting data, using the college laboratory facilities. Each student will keep an accurate lab notebook.

E. Evaluating and interpreting the data and writing a research report.

Each student's progress and performance will be based on discussions with the instructor during class sessions, on the work done in the laboratory, and on the written research proposal and research report. The following criteria will apply:

● Evidence of adequate background knowledge to develop a proposal.

● Evidence of ability to formulate a reasonable and scientifically sound research project and ability to present this project in a clear, well-organized, and appropriate format in the research proposal.

● Ability to apply bioassay techniques and methods in the laboratory.

● Ability to interpret data and results, draw valid conclusions from the results, and ability to present these results and conclusions in a clear, well-organized, and appropriate format in the research report.

Bibliography

Willis H. Johnson, Richard A. Laubengayer, Louis E. Delanney, and Thomas A. Cole, **Biology**

Selected Parts, The Naming and Classification of Animals and Plants, Representative Animals and Animals Phylogeny, Organisms and the Environment

Howard T. Odum, **Fundamentals of Ecology**

U.S. Department of the Interior, **Biology of Water Pollution**

Charles G. Wilber and Charles C. Thomas, **The Biological Aspects of Water Pollution**

J. Cairns, Jr., and K.L. Dickson, **Biological Methods for the Assessment of Water Quality**

U.S. Environmental Protection Agency, **Biological Field and Laboratory Methods for Measuring Quality of Surface Waters and Effluents**

Some Observations

This course includes three of the four major elements of the experiential learning cycle: *observation and reflection, abstract conceptualization,* and *active experimentation.* There is no provision for concrete experiences with significant polluters or pollutants, different toxicity levels, or observable consequences for fish and other animal or plant life. Observation and reflection are restricted to the methods and techniques of the EPA Bioassay Lab. They are not extended to include the political and practical issues involved in selecting sites for collection and analysis and in decisions concerning the disposition and use of reports after the results are in. Both of these elements are important in planning research projects and in preparing reports. They can be significant for the application of research techniques to environmental problems.

• Would the achievement of course objectives be enhanced by beginning with visits to major polluters and polluted waters, by observing the effects of different toxicity levels and different pollutants? Would using water samples from observed sources with pollutants have increased motivation and added useful side effects?

• Would it be useful to have a second research cycle in which students collect samples where toxicity levels and chemical compositions are unknown? Would the subsequent reinforcement and added learning warrant the additional time and costs?

• Would it be possible to make more substantial cooperative arrangements with the EPA and its Bioassay Lab? Could students' research contribute to the work of the Lab? Could students work in close enough relationship with Lab staff and administrators to encounter the practical problems and policy issues involved in carrying out such work? Could such arrangements be made in ways that would result in decreased costs and in more substantial learning?

• Would one or two references concerning the social consequences of water pollution, specific instances of sickness or disease, or examples of degraded lakes or rivers be useful? Would they make more vivid the potential value of the students' learning and the work it makes possible?

The teacher's assumptions about students' prior experiences are not explicit. Perhaps the students already have had direct experiences, or vicarious ones through film or television, that provide a sufficiently rich background for the teacher's starting point. Or perhaps the teacher did not consider that problem or examine those assumptions. All students come with prior experiences. The questions raised here may be significant or irrelevant, depending upon what these experiences have been. It is always helpful to be clear at the outset about prior experiences and the teacher's assumptions.

Race Relations in the United States

The course on Race Relations in the United States had as its major objective "to obtain knowledge of and insight into the history of race relations in the United States during the past 100 years and to acquire concrete impressions of the current situation."

Bibliography

Malcolm X, **Autobiography**
Sig Synnestvedt, **White Response to Black Emancipation**
Eliot M. Rudwick, **Race Riot in East St. Louis**
John Hersey, **Algiers Motel Incident**
Dan T. Carter, **Scottsboro: A Tragedy of the American South**

For each of these books students will prepare a written critique—not more than four pages in length—that will include a single-page synopsis of the book and one to three pages of assessment, evaluation, analysis, judgment, and reaction.

On the basis of these readings, each student will prepare a list of five or six basic questions on white-black relations in the United States. These questions should be designed to get at some basic assumptions about race and about white and black attitudes that may be involved or implicit in these assumptions.

Each student will select 10 persons, 5 white and 5 black, and pose these questions to each in an individual interview session.

Then each student will write a short paper discussing the results of this small collection of impressions. (Note that this assignment is not conceived to be anything more than the collection of a limited set of current impressions that relate to the readings noted above.)

Each student will play the game "Blacks and Whites" for at least an hour with a small group of people, consisting of a mixture of blacks and whites. Cross-assign race roles in advance of starting play, i.e., have some blacks play white roles and vice versa. Write a one- to three-page summary of the results of the game.

Methods and Criteria for Evaluation

Knowledge of the books read will be judged on the quality and accuracy of the written critiques and also by discussion with the teacher. A one-page summary should compress the book, retaining the essential facts and conclusions of the author. They should emerge as a brief but comprehensive outline of the book. The critique should address questions such as: Did the author handle his evidence accurately and fairly? Did he omit important evidence that might have changed his conclusions? What types of evidence did he stress? On a comparative basis, did the author present as convincing a case as the other authors whose work was read for this course or as other authors the student may have read?

Judgment of the student's knowledge of the books and their implications will also be drawn from the nature and quality of the interviews themselves. The questions should demonstrate that the student is aware of such considerations as: differing perceptions and assumptions of blacks and whites in the U.S.; friction-laden experiences of the past; sensitive issues in the present; overall perceptions of progress toward greater and more equal justice or lack of progress toward these goals.

Use of the game "Blacks and Whites" is deliberately designed as a subjective experience without concern for a specific set of outcomes. This experience should be sought at the end of the contract and might be most fruitful if conceived as a means of testing some of the assumptions and perceptions dealt with in the books and revealed in the interviews.

Some Observations

This course encompasses, albeit in somewhat limited fashion, all four elements of experiential learning. Like many courses, it uses varied kinds of literature to supply substitutes for concrete experiences and uses critiques of the literature as vehicles for reflection. As with the previous bioresearch course, the teacher gives no indication of the prior experiences assumed nor makes any direct attempt to ascertain what they might be. The literature may overlap substantially with the experiences of some students and may be completely foreign to others. Would some brief exercise that asked students to examine their past experiences with blacks and whites, or those of their parents and grandparents, be useful prior to plunging into the readings? Would it give the students and the teacher a helpful background for the other course activities?

The formulation of basic questions moves the student to more abstract analyses and syntheses, and the interviews provide not only opportunities for application but also direct experiences with persons who differ from themselves. The paper setting down impressions completes that cycle.

The game "Blacks and Whites" seems to stand somewhat outside the flow of other activities. Yet it can provide experiences that could contribute more directly to the reading, interviews, and reflections. What would have happened if, as a first activity, students played the game in cross-role fashion and set down their understanding of what was going on and why? Then, suppose the game was played again as a final activity and subjected to similar analyses? Would the first and last experiences be different? Would the levels of the analyses change? Would this pre- and postarrangement help students and teacher understand better what has been learned?

One wonders about the racial composition of the class. Assume that both blacks and whites are enrolled. How can students share and compare their different backgrounds to provide added information and experiences? Will the questions they formulate and the impressions they receive from interviews be different? Are there exercises they might undertake that would cast light on principles and issues concerning race relations? When a class contains students from diverse backgrounds, it may also contain rich resources for varied elements of the experiential cycle.

Counseling Theory and Practice

The purpose of this course is (a) to increase students' knowledge of counseling theories, (b) to help them begin to develop their own counseling skills, and (c) to increase their understanding of relationships between counseling and human services and of the social contexts in which they are rendered.

Bibliography

William Glasser, **Reality Therapy**
Joseph Luft, **Introduction to Group Therapy**
Harry Stack Sullivan, **Interpersonal Theory of Psychiatry**
Muriel James and Dorothy Jongeward, **Born to Win**
Erving Goffman, **Asylums**
Abraham Maslow, **Toward a Psychology of Being**
Calvin S. Hall, **A Primer of Freudian Psychology**
Bruce Shertzer and Shelley Stone, **Fundamentals of Counseling**

twenty-five

William Glasser, **Schools Without Failure**
H. Ginsburg and S. Opper, **Piaget's Theory of Intellectual
   Development**
Haim Ginott, **Group Psychotherapy With Children**
C.H. Patterson, **Theories of Counseling and Psychotherapy**
Gordon Allport, **Personality: A Psychological Interpretation**

Students will engage in a series of role-playing exercises designed to aid in understanding initial strengths and weaknesses in counseling techniques. These exercises also will provide an opportunity for students to test the applicability of the counseling techniques they are discovering through their reading. The role plays will be audiotaped and analyzed by student teams with the assistance of the instructor.

Each student will engage in three months of field work in counseling. Several different opportunities will be available and students will choose according to their major interests or future plans. In each of these settings local supervision will be provided. One opportunity involves counseling and training for mothers of newborn infants during their stay in the hospital. This training will include newborn infant care techniques; it also will enable the mother to examine her new role, her personal conflicts, and available social services. Another setting involves counseling obese adolescents and their parents. This counseling will focus on the medical, societal, and psychological implications of the children's obesity. The third setting will involve counseling mothers of children with learning disabilities. This counseling will focus on available medical information, referral opportunities for social services, and parental concerns about themselves and about their children's future.

Student field work also will involve research into community social service facilities and what they require of clients. Students will identify major social service and mental health agencies related to the needs of the persons they counsel. A detailed description of the need requirements, relationships, and activities involved in applying for and receiving services will be created for each agency.

Students will keep journals of their field work activities and their readings. The journal will focus on their encounters with counseling situations and clients. The information will include the techniques used, the student's reaction to the situation, suggestions for improving the counseling situation, and questions on counseling. Through the means of the journal, the students are asked to reflect on and reexamine their personal values. In order to do this, they will maintain ongoing lists of the situations that produce value conflicts within themselves. These will provide a focus for class discussions and for conferences between students and the teacher.

Student learning will be evaluated by means of the written work, the role plays, and discussions as previously enumerated. The development of counseling skills as demonstrated in practice will be evaluated by the supervisor, based on direct observation and on tape recordings. Through these methods, the student is asked to demonstrate the following: (1) an understanding of the counseling theories and techniques contained in each reading; (2) ability to compare each of the theories with the others, focusing on their similarities and dissimilarities; (3) ability to apply counseling techniques in role-play situations and in the student's field work counseling; (4) an increased understanding of social service delivery systems focusing on medical and mental health facilities in particular; (5) ability to synthesize what has been learned in counseling and to apply those learnings in direct case situations; and (6) evidence of a serious exploration of the student's personal values related to counseling and social service work. It should be noted that in addition to the cognitive content of this contract, there is a strong emphasis by the student and mentor on growth in the affective domain.

Some Observations

This course emphasizes the first two steps in experiential learning: *concrete experiences* followed by *observation and reflection*. There is a strong and continuous interplay between these two elements, enriched by readings that bring quite diverse perspectives to bear on the varied counseling opportunities provided.

There is not much emphasis on abstract conceptualization or on explicit application or active experimentation to test generalizations that students might develop. For example, students are not asked to describe the apparent strengths and weaknesses of varied counseling approaches as they apply to the specific persons and situations encountered. There is no overt attempt to bring the student's experience into direct confrontation with the theories in the reading. Nor is there any clear expectation that students might individually articulate their eclectic philosophies or describe the requirements of certain person-situation combinations.

The limited emphasis on abstract conceptualization also is reflected in the activities concerning agency policies and practices. Students might have considered generally the fit between the agencies' espoused theories and the theories in use as expressed by needs, requirements, application processes, and expectations of clients receiving services. General discontinuities between the counselor's assumptions about the person being counseled, the counselor's orientation, and the orientation of different agencies might also have received some systematic attention.

When students are not asked to create larger generalizations, theories, or conceptual frameworks out of the interplay between direct experiences and reflective observations, then the basis for systematic application or experimentation is absent. Such activities therefore cannot occur in any disciplined fashion. Consequently, while there may be substantial increases in competence and knowledge, the foundations on which they rest may remain intuitive.

Early Childhood Education

Early Childhood Education is aimed to help students achieve the following objectives:

1. To understand the needs of educationally and socially deprived children, the kinds of curricular enrichment called for, and the kinds of testing procedures that may be useful.

2. To gain knowledge of the establishment, administration, operation, curriculum, and educational practices of a day care center.

3. To study innovative alternatives that might be applied to improve the quality of day care programs.

To work toward these objectives:

1. Each student will participate for a minimum of two full mornings a week as a teacher's aide in one of the community day care centers. Students will work with children who require individual attention in language enrichment, reading readiness, social skills, and motivation. Students also will work with small groups of children on cooking projects to teach the

language of new foods, utensils, and cooking processes; the mathematical skills involved in measuring and weighing; and the social skills involved in a cooperative effort. The students also will teach songs, games, and finger play poems. They will research preschool books available for reading to children and will practice reading to small groups of children. In addition, they will work with children who want to use the books for dramatic play.

2. Each student will research testing programs for children three to five years of age and design a program appropriate for that center to determine the intellectual performance of each child. Students will use these tests to obtain information about the communication skills, perceptual development, and knowledge of basic concepts demonstrated by five-year-olds, four-year-olds, and three-year-olds. This work will be done under the supervision of the director.

3. The student will participate with the staff in planning sessions and will study literature on curriculum design and program planning generally applicable to day care centers and pertinent to the particular center at hand. Lesson plans will be created in the areas of language development and learning readiness, submitted to the director, and carried out as part of the curriculum if feasible and approved by the director.

4. Students will attend seminars and meetings of the Association for Education of Young Children and read pertinent literature such as *The Voice for Children; Learning;* and the *Journal of the National Association for Education of Young Children.*

5. Once each month the student will spend a full day at the center to observe the problems in planning and carrying out a full day's program.

6. Each student will research innovative programs that might be applicable to day care centers and, whenever possible, will visit other centers using innovative programs. This research will include study of television programs such as "Sesame Street," "The Electric Company," and cartoon programs as a source of useful ideas.

7. Each student will keep a weekly log of activities at the center, meetings, and readings. Basic readings pertinent to general objectives of the course and to particular issues students may encounter are available from the attached bibliography.

8. Each student will submit a final paper to the center director, with a copy to the instructor, analyzing the center operation and outlining any innovations or recommendations which may seem appropriate. The analyses and recommendations will be supported not only by the student's own observations but by references to pertinent principles, theories, or research findings provided in the literature.

9. The director of the day care center, its teachers, and its staff all will serve as resource persons for aides, who are expected to use their initiative to make use of these resources. If problems arise that cannot be resolved, the instructors stand ready to help.

Student performance will be evaluated as follows:

1. The student's weekly log will be reviewed periodically and will serve as a framework for ongoing evaluation. The consistency of effort, the level of responsibility, and the integrity of reporting will be taken into account at the point of final evaluation.

2. Students will incorporate past research in early childhood development, educational theories regarding early childhood learning, and educational psychology with their practical experiences. The primary evidence for this knowledge will be their contributions as active members of the day care center staff. Skill in working with the children and the ability to help them in their intellectual and emotional development will be observed and evaluated by the director and the instructor. This evaluation

will make use of the lesson plans and of the contributions to curriculum design and program planning.

3. Both the director and the instructor will evaluate the student's analytic paper and recommendations for improving the center operation. They will look for the degree to which the student identifies critical problem areas and is able to apply pertinent information from the literature to recommendations for change.

Bibliography

Verna Hildebrand, **Introduction to Early Childhood Education**
Susan W. Gray, **Before First Grade**
S. Alan Cohen, **Teach Them All to Read: Theory, Methods, and Materials for Teaching the Disadvantaged**
Tina E. Bangs, **Language and Learning Disorders of the Pre-Academic Child**
Dennis McFadden, Ed., **Planning for Action: Early Childhood Development Programs and Services**
Else Hauessermann, **Developmental Potential of Preschool Children**
Fred M. Hechinger, Ed., **Preschool Education Today**
Vivian E. Todd and Helen Heffernan, **The Years Before School**
Robert C. Augerman, **Approaches to Beginning Reading**
Carl Bereiter and Siegfried Englemann, **Teaching Disadvantaged Children in Preschool**
Ruth Hamlin, **Schools for Young Disadvantaged Children**
Gerald S. Lesser, **Learning, Teaching, and Television Production for Children: The Experiment of Sesame Street**
Wilbur Schramm, et al., **Television in the Lives of Our Children**
Julian C. Stanley, Ed., **Preschool Programs for the Disadvantaged: Five Experimental Approaches**

Some Observations

This course encompasses all the ingredients of experiential learning. Each student's weekly work as a teacher's aide calls for substantial immersion in diverse experiences and varied responsibilities. These experiences are enlarged by periodic attendance at seminars and meetings of the Association for Education of Young Children. The weekly log provides a framework for observations and reflections and for articulating relationships with pertinent readings. The readings are not substitutes for direct experiences but become sources of insight and information that students can use to increase their understanding of the children and of the situations they encounter and to increase their competence in relation to responsibilities they assume.

The development of general concepts and abstract principles occurs in the service of immediate application to the needs of the day care center. The cycle from abstract conceptualization to concrete application or active experimentation, in the context of ongoing direct experiences, occurs in three areas: testing, curriculum, and lesson plans for teaching.

The experiences and idiosyncrasies of the particular center in which a student works are amplified by visits to other centers searching for helpful innovations and by scanning the media and other sources of ideas. A closing perspective on the whole experience is provided by the final paper analyzing the center and making recommendations for its improvement.

There is ample opportunity for continuous formative evaluation. By the end of the semester the quality of the performance and the nature of the summative evaluation should be clear to the student, the teacher, and the center supervisor and staff. There should be few surprises in store for anyone, and the student should have a sound basis for making judgments about future learning and future employment. In this case, a student's prior experience and competence will be quickly revealed during the early stages of work at the center. Responsibilities, readings, and writings can then be managed and evaluated accordingly.

An Individual Contract in Human Services and Criminal Justice

A. *Student's General Purposes*
    1. Academic Purpose: BA degree and preparation for graduate program in social work.
    2. Vocational Purpose: Direct practice in social work profession.
B. *Specific Purposes*
    1. I wish to obtain an overview of various human services, as an intervention medium, to deal with social problems.
    2. I wish to acquire skills in social work practice, to try out social work practice roles in the field, and to test in a field setting theories and principles learned.
    3. I will explore the American prison system from a sociological, psychological, economic, and political viewpoint.
C. *Learning Activities*
    1. Readings on criminal justice (as per attached open-ended bibliography).
    2. Visit with Friends of Fortune.
    3. Visit with legal aid and law services.
    4. STEP (Service Training Education Program) of Family Service Association (FSA) of Nassau County.
        a. Classroom seminars begin October 2, 1977—one morning per week.
        b. Field work placement commitment of two to two and one half days per week in FSA programs such as Debt Counseling, Information and Referral, Senior Citizens, and Family Advocacy.
D. *Evaluation*
    1. Regular weekly meeting with mentor.
    2. Written reports and participation in seminars.
    3. Peer and supervisory conferences.
    4. Log of field experiences as a learning activity.
    5. Research paper that will attempt to integrate and critically consider the body of ideas learned in study of the American prison system.

Bibliography

Harry Elmer Barnes, **The Story of Punishment**
Harry Elmer Barnes and Negley K. Teeters, **New Horizons in Criminology**
Janet Harris, **Crisis in Corrections—The Prison Problem**
Milton Haynes and Herman Badillo, **A Bill of No Rights: Attica and the American Prison System**
George Jackson, **Soledad Brother, The Letters of G. Jackson**
Karl Menninger, M.D., **The Crime of Punishment**
Jessica Mitford, **Kind and Usual Punishment: The Prison Business**
Robert W. Peterson, Ed., **Crime and the American Response**

Piri Thomas, **Seven Long Times**
Harleigh B. Trecker, **Social Group Work**
Erik Olin Wright, **The Politics of Punishment: A Critical Analysis of Prisons in America**
H.J. Griswold, Mike Misenheimer, Art Powers, and Ed Tromanhauser, **An Eye for an Eye: Four Inmates of the Crime of American Prisons Today**

Some Observations

This is a terse contract, but it includes substantial and well-integrated experiential learning. The student's purposes explicitly aim to test theories and principles in the field, and that is carried out in the context of classroom seminars that should provide opportunities to reflect on the field experiences. Visits to pertinent agencies provide further direct experience. Only the objective concerning the American prison system is left at the level of observations and reflection supplied by readings. Abstract conceptualization is provided by a research paper. No direct observation of prisoners or prisons is stipulated, no field work activities with prisoners or their families are contemplated, unless they are to occur in the context of the FSA field work placement.

There is no indication of the student's level of prior experience or knowledge, but this would have been explored and understood by both parties in the process of developing the contract, as initial purposes were defined and the learning activities identified. The field experience log, the peer and supervisory conferences, the seminar reports and participation, and the weekly meetings with the mentor give this contract a solid range of formative evaluation activities as the work goes forward. Summative evaluation, therefore, will rest on a rich body of information and final judgments about the quality of performance should contain few surprises.

An Individual Contract in Agriculture and Woodworking

A. *Student's General Purposes*
My purpose is to obtain a BA degree with a concentration in "The Ecology of Integral Being." In pursuing my lifelong study of how to maximize consciousness in all areas of my life, I am completing my degree through deepening and balancing my learning in agriculture and woodworking.
B. *Specific Purposes*
    1. Relative to agriculture: To become familiar with methods of pruning and training deciduous fruit trees.
    2. *Relative to Woodworking*
        a. To gain experience with the tongue-and-groove method of carcase construction and drawer work. To seek increased exactitude and make observations on the process of small-scale production of a hand-crafted item.
        b. Facility is sought with the tools employed in faceplate turning by producing numerous bowls of varying shapes and sizes in different woods.
C. *Learning Activities*
    1. *Agriculture*
        a. Various texts and visual aids will be employed to

study techniques and systems of pruning.

b._____ of the New York Experiment Station at Geneva has agreed to instruct me in aspects of pruning.

c. Additional visits to the orchards of nearby fruit growers may be undertaken.

d. Practical experience will be gained through the application of the above learnings in an available orchard with trees of varying ages.

2. *Woodworking*

a. Working in conjunction with another craftsman of the Rochester Folk Art Guild, the student will undertake to produce 10 small pine drawer chests with tongue-and-grooved sides, paneled back, mortise and tenon rails, three drawers, and turned apple wood drawer pulls.

b. The student will attempt to turn 6 walnut bowls approximately 8" in diameter, 6 maple bowls approximately 9" in diameter, and 12 cherry bowls approximately 4" in diameter.

D. *Evaluation*

1. Evaluation of pruning will be done by_____ by examining the orchard upon completion of my work.

2. Evaluation of woodworking will be done by_____, head of the woodshop of the Rochester Folk Art Guild. Criteria will be demonstrated acquisition of increased skill and artisanship.

Some Observations

Many things cannot be learned without concrete experience and active practice. This is true of most skills, crafts, arts, sports, foreign languages, and many vocational and professional activities ranging from auto mechanics to surgery. Some of our heady learning theories, which concentrate on what goes on inside the brain, neglect the fact that many kinds of learning depend heavily on developing perceptual sensitivities with the eyes, ears, fingers, and even with nostrils. They depend also on highly tuned small and large muscle coordination.

In such learning, abstract conceptualization usually plays a limited role and sometimes actually seems to hamper learning and performance. That is the message of *Zen and the Art of Archery* and of *The Inner Game of Tennis.* Good athletes recognize that they are off their game when they have to start thinking and talking themselves through the moves. In this kind of learning, the key loop goes from direct experience through observation and application and then back again to direct experience. The important point is to keep that cycle going.

This contract, therefore, with its limited emphasis on abstract conceptualization and its strong emphasis on experience, observation, and practice, makes obvious sense. You can be shown quite easily how to cut a branch off a tree so the bark doesn't rip and so it will heal quickly. But distinguishing a well-pruned tree from a butchered one is something else again. Knowing which combinations of branches will result in what shape, for what purposes, evolves only after tackling a significant number of different kinds of trees and the singular problems each presents. In theory, it is simple to saw a square corner, create a tight joint, turn a well-proportioned bowl. In practice, it is not so easy—as any do-it-yourselfer will testify.

One of the nice things about such learning is that feedback and evaluation are usually concrete, continuous, and unequivocal. Sometimes an outside opinion is required, but usually the results are perfectly, if not painfully, clear. Perhaps there are other less obvious types of learning where our academic emphasis on reflection and abstract conceptualization has led us to ignore significant areas of perceptual sensitivity and neuromuscular skill.

An Individual Contract in Environmental Studies

A. *General Purposes*
My major interest is toward environmental studies with a holistic approach. I intend to learn all I can so that I, as an individual, and we, as human beings, can live on this earth in a more humane and ecologically sound way.

B. *Specific Purposes*
Specifically, I will be studying alternate technological systems: the hardware and the software. Alternate technological systems may briefly be defined as alternatives to present technological systems, alternatives that recognize the need for developing a limited, or controlled-growth, or even a nongrowth economy as well as the need for creating a more humane, less destructive society. The hardware includes just that: windmills, methane generators, low-cost, low-energy housing, etc. The software includes the philosophy, the attitudes, the values people possess in conjunction with designing and building these systems.

One of the major questions of this study will be: Can the "new technology" not only help free humanity from want of material goods and needless toil but can it also help us develop a way of life that will enable us to live in harmony with our fellow human beings, with nature, and with the natural laws of the cosmos? Other questions to be explored are: What does the "new technology" entail in terms of its hardware and software (in their technological, social, political, economic, and philosophical aspects)? Why and how is this technology emerging?

Other interests I wish to explore are photography and travel, especially by means of hitchhiking. In my study of alternate technological systems, therefore, I will be traveling to different places where people are doing work on these types of systems. The places and the people who work and/or live there will be one of my major resources. Besides the intrinsic value of my study of photography, taking photos will be one of the ways for me to document my learning for this contract.

C. *Learning Activities*
1. I will read a number of books and articles that pertain to the hardware as well as the social, political, economic, philosophical, and purely technological aspects of the emerging new planetary culture. (See bibliography.)
2. P. Soleri, archologist and visionary, holds workshops on his conception of archologies (centralized structures for human habitation that combine architecture with ecology) in Arizona. I have been accepted for the workshop session beginning August 12, 1977, and I will participate in this session full time until September 30, 1977.
3. Travel is in itself a learning activity. Much of this study

will include travel, and much of this travel will be done by hitchhiking. I believe I am a competent traveler when it comes to the United States. I have been on cross-country camping trips to the Southwest and California, as well as in the northeastern U.S. and Canada. I have taken a 700-mile bicycle trip from Long Island to Cape Cod and have hitchhiked to California twice, as well as to Florida and parts of Canada. I have not only learned a great deal from travel itself but also from hitchhiking. Others may consider such rides incidental, but I believe hitchhiking is an extraordinary educational venture, a good way of learning about a society and its culture. I have found some of the people who have given me rides to be phenomenal educational resources. I therefore plan to travel by hitching across the United States from New York to Wisconsin; on to California by way of Colorado, Utah, and Nevada; down the coast of California from San Francisco to San Diego; and then over to Arizona for the workshops. My travels may also include camping and backpacking in areas such as national parks and forests, including the Big Sur area of California, and climbing Mt. Whitney in the High Sierras.

I intend to keep a journal of my travel experiences and of my encounters with people and places. I also plan to read such books as the following: *The Hitchhikers Handbook* (Tom Grim); *On the Road* (Jack Kerouac); *Kerouac* (Ann Charters); *The Electric Koolaid Acid Test* (Tom Wolfe); and *Howl* and *Reality Sandwiches* (Alan Ginsberg).

4. To facilitate my study of alternate technological systems, I plan to visit the following places to talk with resource people who are doing work on such systems, according to this approximate schedule:

a. Late June to early July: The New Alchemist—East (Woods Hole, Massachusetts). This is a small, international organization for research and education toward ecological and social transformations. The people there conceive of their task as the creation of ecologically derived forms of energy, agriculture, aquaculture, housing, and landscapes that permit revitalization of the countryside.

b. July 10-14: The University of Wisconsin: I plan to investigate their program of research with methane digesters and solar heating.

c. July 16-20: camping in the Rocky Mountains and High Sierras.

d. July 25-26: The University of California at Santa Barbara, Santa Cruz, and Berkeley: I will check out their ecology centers and environmental programs and visit a community farming project (as well as evaluate the potential for my future study there).

e. Last week in July: The New Alchemist Institute—West. I will study their methane digesters and techniques for generating electricity with wind power.

f. Last week in July: I will visit _____ in San Diego; he is a designer/inventor.

5. I have pursued the study of photography on my own and have had some darkroom experience. In order to develop my understanding of the art of photography, I shall make a

photographic documentary of the places I visit. Upon return-
ing to New York, I will try to get more darkroom experience
and will consult with my mentor for assistance.

D. *Methods of Evaluation*

1. Along with a personal journal, I shall keep a collection of
notes summarizing what I have learned from the various people and places I will visit. This notebook of learning experiences, as well as my narrative journal on traveling experiences
described above, will be submitted to my mentor.

2. I will also prepare a photographic journal, using some
suggestions from the mentor, and will submit such a journal
to him for evaluation of my photographic and darkroom
learning.

3. I will correspond biweekly with my mentor, keeping him
well informed of my activities and consulting with him on
study-related problems for his advice and assistance.

4. Letters of evaluation from my workshop leader as well as
from qualified people at the places I visit will be sent to my
mentor.

5. An annotated bibliography of my readings will be prepared and given to my mentor for evaluation.

E. *Bibliography*

Each place I visit has its own collection of written materials. Much of the
material I shall read (especially magazine articles) cannot be cited here in
advance. The following is a partial list of books I will read:

Bibliography

Sandi Eccli, Ed., **Alternative Sources of Energy: Book One**
Bruce Anderson, **Solar Energy and Shelter Design**
John Hold and Philip Herra, **Energy**
N.Y.S. Interdept. of Fuel and Energy Committee, **Appliance
and Apparatus Efficiency**
Paolo Soleri, **Archology: City in the Image of Man**
Ian McHarg, **Design With Nature**
Garrett DeBell, Ed., **Environmental Handbook**
William Irwin Thomson, **Passages About Earth: An Explora-
tion of the New Planetary Culture**
John McHale, **The Future of the Future**
Marshall McLuhan and Quentin Fiore, **The Medium Is the
Message**
The Last Whole Earth Catalog
Victor Papanek, **Design for the Real World**
Paul Goodman and Percival Goodman, **Communitas**
Murray Bookchin, **Post-Scarcity Anarchism**
William Hedgepath and Dennis Stock, **The Alternative: Com-
munal Life in America**
F.D. Emery, **Systems Thinking**
Ansel Adams, **Camera and Lens**
David Brower, **Only a Little Planet**
John Muir, **Gentle Wilderness: The Sierra Nevada**

Some Observations

Oh to be young again! Wouldn't you love to do that contract? Especially with some judiciously spaced motel stops for a hot tub, a good
bed, and a shot of Cronkite? It is reminiscent of a nineteenth century
grand tour. Maybe you are not interested in environmental problems and alternatives for low energy and renewable resources. But
this student obviously is and already knows a lot about it—and he
has thought about it carefully in terms of experiential learning.

We can anticipate some of the major problems. The most critical probably will be self-discipline concerning the annotated bibliography, the biweekly correspondence with the mentor, and the personal journal—in that order. The heavy involvement with the people and places visited, the sensuality, the flexibility, the practical problems that make being on the road so attractive, are not conducive to systematic observation and reflection. Even skilled use of the camera provides only a limited approximation. Abstract conceptualizations only trivialize, distort, demean. Perhaps this person will be able to accept the compromises and will have the required self-discipline, but it will not be easy. Without systematic use of the readings, the correspondence, and the journal, the educational value of the experiences will be diminished and solid evaluation of the contract will be very difficult.

The next three contracts—in sociology, mental health and retardation services, and American studies—are presented without comment. You may have been making your own observations concerning the earlier courses and contracts, and they may be in disagreement with mine. Now you can do your own analyses and make your own observations uncontaminated by the author's. How do these contracts exemplify or depart from Coleman's steps or Kolb's experiential learning cycle? What are their strengths and weaknesses? What would you add, omit, or do differently?

Obviously, our observations are limited by the fact that most of us do not have professional expertise in these three areas, but perhaps we have some useful ideas. In any event, no one is going to grade the responses. The main object here is simply to begin using some of these ideas concerning experiential learning as a route to further understanding and as a warmup for more thorough application.

An Individual Contract in Sociology

A. *Student's General Purpose*
The general purpose of the works undertaken at Empire State College is to fulfill the degree requirements for a BA degree in sociology. This contract is the first of a series of learning activities designed to develop proficiency in sociological research procedures and methods.
B. *Specific Purposes*
The specific purposes of this contract will be to:
    1. Develop an outline for a publishable document that will address the lifestyles, norms, values, and problems of the black aged.
    2. To undertake independent course work to acquire learning equal to the curriculum defined in the traditional course entitled Social Stratification.
C. *Learning Activities*
The learning activities that will be pursued to fulfill the goals of this contract are:
    1. Readings in sociology that will include a survey of the related literature to determine the social, economic, and political opportunity structure available to blacks between 1900 and 1917.
    2. An analysis of the 1960 census to determine the social, economic, and political characteristics of black Americans,

and the status of the 1974 aged during preretirement years.

3. An analysis of the 1973 census to determine the social, economic, and political characteristics of black Americans as they relate to the 1960 census and the black aged.

4. Interviews with 10 black, elderly people born between 1870 and 1917 to obtain a historical collective overview of their perceived opportunities and lifestyles.

5. Interviews with 10 white, elderly people born between 1870 and 1917 to obtain a historical collective overview of their perceived opportunities and lifestyles.

6. Conduct a study of the class structure: a review of objective and subjective approaches, the relationship of status, class, and power.

D. *Mentor Evaluation*

1. The major focus of the learning contract is to generate a sociological analysis of the black elderly in the United States. The products will be an outline of the potentially publishable document addressing the issues cited above and some sample chapters. The work will be evaluated by the mentor with special attention to the level of analysis presented, the ability to understand and employ theory, the ability to interpret and generate sociological data, and the ability to present a logical, coherent, sociological exposition.

An Individual Contract in Mental Health and Retardation Services

A. *Student's General Purpose*

To obtain a BS degree with a concentration in community psychology.

B. *Specific Purposes*

1. Achieve an understanding of the unified services approach and other future forms of mental health and retardation services.

2. Apply a variety of skills, knowledge, and concepts related to human services planning and administration in managing a volunteer group.

3. Acquire knowledge of the state education department's position and recent legislation related to the education of children with handicapping conditions.

C. *Learning Activities*

1. Attend the local conference where William Goldman, commissioner of the Massachusetts Department of Mental Health, lectures on his experiences in mental health services. Review the New York State unified services law and guidelines. Prepare and submit a summary of findings.

2. As chairperson of the Monroe County Coordinating Group on Mental Retardation conduct the duties required of this office. Discuss with the mentor the activities undertaken and submit any documents prepared while serving in this capacity.

3. Collect recent documents on the education of children with handicapping conditions, attend any local clarification meeting, and submit a summary of findings to the mentor.

4. Participate in the workshop entitled Planning and Implementation of Comprehensive Human Services. Prepare a re-

port addressing the workshop content and the applicability of the concepts and techniques learned. The report should have an objective, critical, professional point of view.

D. *Methods and Criteria for Evaluation*

1. The summary of future forms of mental health and retardation services will be evaluated for its clarity and comprehensiveness.

2. The activities undertaken as chairperson of the Monroe County Coordinating Group on Mental Retardation will be evaluated for the extent to which they represent the use of management skills, knowledge and concepts formerly acquired, and their effectiveness in bringing about change.

3. The summary of findings on New York State's position on the education of children with handicapping conditions will be evaluated for its representation of understanding of the intent and issues involved.

4. The workshop report will be evaluated for its clarity, objectivity, and professional criticism.

An Individual Travel Contract in American Studies

Student's General Purposes

Ms._____will be working toward a BA degree with concentration in American studies. She wants to learn about this country—its social, political, economic, and religious forces; its myths; its history and its future—and she wants to understand her place within American culture. She seeks to learn about the various influences of the culture upon her: institutional, scientific, technological, attitudinal/ideological. She wants, in turn, to develop and direct her talents and interests in order to have some personal impact upon this culture.

Specific Purposes of This Contract

My first contract will be a new start in a new environment, with different circumstances and a change in lifestyle involving unfamiliar people. It will therefore be necessary to know where I'm starting from and where I've been, and to understand the past.

(Self-definition) My experiences in the western United States will challenge my ideas, knowledge, and attitudes. This testing of my past and of myself will cause revision and self-growth.

(Awareness) Defining myself and understanding my personal growth will help me to clarify my purposes and to gain some directions.

The quality that I most hope to consider and develop is independence. I want to prove that (1) I can take care of, provide for, and think for myself; and (2) I want to feel what it's like to be on my own, without familiar people for a while. This is the way to understand and determine how I feel about my friends and anyone else I have dealings with, and to determine where I belong.

Two skills I hope to develop and maintain are examination and reevaluation. New experiences will create many opportunities for these skills to flourish. Eventually, I hope to reach a period of stabilization.

I expect to gain a knowledge of cultural aspects of America and particularly of California: history, geography, politics, religion, sociology.

Learning Activities

The central learning activity of this contract will be the student's journal of exploration. In this journal she will record, reflect upon, and eventually try to integrate the dynamics and directions and the growth of her ideas and feelings about herself and her goals and about California as an experience of American culture.

The following readings are intended to suggest various models for conceptualization: for observation, analysis, organization, and articulation of the student's learning experiences. The purpose of these readings is for the student to begin to develop a critical perspective and methodology for her own use in exploring American culture. In studying selections from each of the following categories, the student will consider questions such as these:

What models for observation and thought does this work/ form provide?

What kinds of perception and awareness are predominant in this work/form?

What facets of experience is the writer able to express through this form?

How does the form shape the experience presented?

On theories of culture: What definitions and conceptual frameworks of culture does this writer provide?

What ideas and what kinds of data are central to this concept?

How and to what extent might this form/model be useful to me in analyzing, conceptualizing, organizing, and articulating my own questions, problems, ideas, and experiences of California and of American culture in general?

Bibliography

Travel Journals
  Henry David Thoreau, **Cape Cod**
  Francis Parkman, **Oregon Trail**
Travel Fiction
  Homer, **The Odyssey**
  Herman Melville, **Typee**
  Jack Kerouac, **On the Road**
  John Steinbeck, **Travels With Charley**
  Judith Rossner, **Any Minute I Can Split**
Fiction About the California Experience
  Gertrude Atherton, **The Splendid, Idle Forties; The Californians**
  Nathaniel West, **The Day of the Locust**
  Thomas Pynchon, **The Crying of Lot 49**
Studies Based on On-Site Observation
  James Agee, **Let Us Now Praise Famous Men**
  Elliot Liebow, **Talley's Corner**
  Sharon Curtin, **Nobody Ever Died of Old Age**
  Emily Bowen, **Return to Laughter**
Cultural Study Concepts and Methodology
  Peter L. Berger and Thomas Luckmann, **Social Construction of Reality**
  E.T. Hall, **Hidden Dimension**
  Anthony Wallace, **Culture and Personality**
  Robert Merton, **On Theoretical Sociology**
  C. Wright Mills, **Sociological Imagination; Power Elite**
  Leslie White, **Science of Culture**
California: Its Place in American Culture
  Kevin Starr, **Americans and the California Dream**
  Neil Morgan, **The California Syndrome**
  Robert Durrenberger, **California: The Last Frontier**

Methods and Criteria of Evaluation
The student will present her learnings from this contract in the following manner: She will write separate accounts of her experience in California using each of the forms studied in this contract. Thus she will be submit-

ting a travel journal (or sample portions), a piece of on-the-road fiction, a story about California, an on-site observation, and a series of essays (at least three) on California, based upon some of the conceptual frameworks of culture study encountered in her readings. In writing these various accounts she will be free to draw upon all facets and all levels of her learning experiences.

Finally, she will submit an overall essay analyzing the uses and potential of each of these forms, i.e., How much and what facets of her experience was she able to express using a given form or conceptual framework? What parts of her experience could she not express through a given form or conceptual framework? Which approaches were most valuable to her in stimulating thought and awareness, in helping to make conceptual sense of her experience, in leading her to greater depth or breadth of inquiry? Were there facets of her experience (impressions, feelings, ideas, questions) that she could not explore or express using any of these forms or frameworks? If so, what were they? Was she able to find or create another form or framework of her own to deal with these facets of her experience?

Application and Experimentation

So far I have tried in a limited way to incorporate three elements of the experiential learning cycle: abstract conceptualizations from Coleman and Kolb, concrete examples of some courses and contracts, observations and reflections concerning those examples. It would be useful, and it would lend a certain symmetry, to apply these ideas and experiences by designing your own course or contract. We do not usually expect to do this when we sit down to read. If we are put off by the suggestion, it may help us recognize—in a minor but explicit way—a fundamental problem with experiential learning. It requires active participation and engagement. It is not satisfied by passively absorbing another person's ideas. When we ask students to undertake experiential learning, we may find similar reactions of surprise, disinclination, or active resistance. You could take an individual student, a recent course or one coming up, or yourself and something you want to learn. If you are an administrator and none of these alternatives seems appropriate, you might design a professional development program for other administrators or for faculty members.

Construct a plan that makes use of these ideas concerning experiential learning and your own added insights. Describe the purposes or objectives. Indicate the information available about the prior experiences or knowledge shared by the learners or the assumptions you make about them. Lay out the activities to be undertaken, making conscious decisions about the use of concrete experiences, observation and reflection, abstract conceptualization, and active experimentation. Then describe how the learning will be evaluated in relation to the purposes or objectives. What evidence will be available? What methods will be used? What criteria will determine success or failure? Who will be responsible?

Perhaps this Experiential Learning Analyzer will help. It is not exhaustive, and it certainly is not final—so revise at will.

1. What experiences and knowledge do the students bring?
   Have they had direct experiences pertinent to this area?

Have they acquired relevant information, insights, principles, concepts?

Have they had opportunities to apply or experiment with pertinent concepts and principles?

2. Where is the best place to begin?

Are direct experiences necessary before introducing abstract principles?

Do students' current or recent experiences provide a basis for starting with observations and reflections?

Is it best to start with basic principles or concepts that will help students make sense of prior or ongoing experiences?

Is it best to start with immediate application and experimentation in order to generate direct experiences that can then provide building blocks for reflection and abstract conceptualization?

3. What kinds of experiences would be most pertinent?

Are direct experiences practically accessible?

Are there vicarious experiences available through print, pictures, simulations, artistic productions, and the like?

4. What kinds of tools or procedures for observation and reflection would be most appropriate?

Photographs, recordings, written descriptions?

Diaries, logs, free associations, periodic reactions?

Small group discussions, dyadic exchanges, individual or group presentations?

5. What are the best ways to generate abstract concepts, principles, general understandings?

Are textbooks and secondary sources most appropriate?

Are there original writings that connect more directly?

Can they be induced from individual students, from subgroups, or from the total group?

6. What are the possibilities for application and active experimentation?

Can hypotheses be generated and tested through empirical research?

Can general principles be tested in action so that observable results are obtained?

7. Are there clear relationships among the direct experiences, reflections and observations, abstract conceptualizations, and applications?

What activities will help students perceive and examine those relationships?

How might written papers, metaphors, pictorial or dramatic presentations, or action plans help create an effective integration?

8. Does evaluation take account of direct experiences and active applications as well as observations, reflections, and abstract conceptualizations?

Do the arrangements for ongoing "formative" evaluation examine both the separate elements of the experiential learning cycle and the relationships among them?

Does the final "summative" evaluation examine the level of integration achieved between the concrete experiences and application and the reflections and abstract conceptualizations?

In formulating these plans, be as explicit as you can concerning actual settings, responsibilities, activities, supervisors, readings, writings, time expectations, and the like. If you push yourself to be as detailed as possible, then you will reach a level where the problems and potentials in your particular circumstances will become more apparent. While you are creating this design for experiential learning, make a list of (a) the problems and difficulties you or the learners would encounter trying to put this plan in place and carry it out, and (b) the advantages, if any, over the approaches currently used. With these concepts, examples, observations, and applications in hand, and with some sense of the problems and advantages that might characterize particular situations, we now have a sufficient basis for considering problems and potentials, costs and policy implications.

3

Problems: Purposes,
Substance, and Quality

TAKEN SERIOUSLY, EXPERIENTIAL LEARNING CAN RAISE
fundamental questions concerning institutional purposes and orientation: Is the education we offer really useful? And useful for what?
Are we concerned about helping students develop professional and
vocational skills and prepare more generally for the world of work?
Just what is the role of the liberal arts? Can we create effective combinations of liberal learning and professional training?

If we were to begin to recognize the range of knowledge, abilities,
and personal characteristics required to function effectively on the
job, at home, and in the community, just where would we stop with
educational designs? Would we then presume to meet all the needs
of all persons, for whatever settings they might want to tackle? Interpersonal competence is obviously a key requirement—but can
we teach it, evaluate it, or even define it? And if we take the step
into the "affective domain," what about questions of autonomy and
interdependence, moral and ethical development, issues of value
and social action?

What do we mean by "learning"? What do we accept as evidence
that it has, in fact, occurred? If someone can *do* a thing, is that
enough? If someone can *talk* about how to do something, is that
enough? Would we be so bold as to require both? Which kinds of
learning are best demonstrated by doing and which by conceptualizing? If we add to our courses learning demonstrated by performance in experiential settings—on a job, in a volunteer activity,
through a field project—then can we ignore such evidence when a
new student comes to us and asks that it be credited? What is "college-level learning" anyway? How can we define it for these new
areas of competence and knowledge, demonstrated by evidence for
which we have no prior standards or conventions?

Such questions with regard to institutional purposes and their relation to the larger social context, to the range of learning we can responsibly assist, to the evidence we will accept and the standards we will use, are all implicit in serious attempts to move toward experiential learning. A college or university needs to be self-conscious and clear about its answers. Many institutions, of course, have given hard thought to such matters in any case, and a debate over experiential learning can be the occasion for a similar effort.

Learning usually proceeds best when both students and teacher are clear about relationships between objectives and activities designed to serve them. Teachers and students should know what to expect from reading a book, writing a paper, preparing for an essay or multiple-choice examination—or what can be accomplished in a lecture, seminar, or group discussion. When teaching and learning are encompassed by these familiar bounds, we set objectives and expectations, albeit modestly, with some confidence that we know what they mean and that we can achieve them.

But we also recognize that there are significant interactions between means and ends, between purposes and the activities used to pursue them. When those activities include significant encounters with persons of different race, economic class, or social background, through counseling, teaching, interviewing, volunteer activities, or shared work—who can say what outcomes may result? How can either a student or a teacher anticipate what may happen when a concerned person observes, close up, the gaps between the espoused theories of a health or welfare agency and its actual practices and effects, and the gap between the needs of a client and what is actually received? When our environmental and American studies students hit the road, can they really predict where that road will take them?

These intrusive imponderables can stop us in our tracks when we try to establish objectives and expectations for students and ourselves. Should we recognize larger possibilities concerning self-understanding, self-determination, social awareness and social action, values and attitude change? Should we encourage students to address those possibilities more explicitly? Or should we simply note such fancies in passing, or ignore them and concentrate on more immediate objectives? The courses and contracts examined earlier are generally cautious and conservative in their objectives. They emphasize cognitive results (and basic ones at that) concerned with knowledge acquisition and comprehension: "to gain experience and knowledge in bioassay techniques," "to obtain knowledge and insight into the history of race relations," "to increase knowledge of counseling theories...to develop counseling skills...to understand relationships between human services and the social context," "to understand the needs of educationally deprived children."

These are all traditional cognitive objectives. There is nothing wrong with them, but they are limited. They do not even reach for more complex cognitive outcomes concerning application, analysis, synthesis, and evaluation. These courses and contracts, however, will yield learning beyond the basic knowledge acquired. They will require more complex intellectual skills. Successful achievement also will call for interpersonal competence, social sensitivity, expressive skills, and emotional maturity.

Some students and teachers do venture further. One student defined a degree with a concentration in "the ecology of integral being" as part of a lifelong effort "to maximize consciousness in all areas of my life." This student and teacher see contributions that woodworking, cabinetmaking, and pruning and training trees can make to that complex, idealistic purpose. Another student pursues environmental studies "so that I as an individual and we as human beings can live on this earth in a more humane and ecologically sound way." What, then, is the specific purpose here? "Can the 'new technology' not only help free humanity from want of material goods and needless toil, but can it also help us develop a way of life that will enable us to live in harmony with our fellow human beings, with nature, and with the natural laws of the cosmos?" Is this an acceptable learning objective? Good luck! The American studies student "wants to understand her place within American culture... seeks to learn about the various influences of the culture upon her... wants, in turn, to develop and direct her own talents and interests in order to have some personal impact upon this culture."

Are far-reaching purposes such as these legitimate and realizable? Is there any way on earth, or elsewhere, that progress or achievement can be assessed? Should we even try? What are the limits we set on what we might hope to accomplish responsibly? How do we define these limits when we help students tackle experiences that are clearly related to such large purposes and that have powerful potentials for learning and personal development?

Of course there are books, films, lectures, and personal contacts with professors and fellow students, which provoke similarly far-reaching changes. We recognize them when they happen, but we do not usually assume such consequences for many students. Nor do we build such expectations into course objectives. Adding concrete experiences, active application, and experimentation raises these questions anew; advancing judgments that seem sound and reasonable make for a challenging task.

These problems concerning purposes take us quickly to questions of substance and quality. Educational quality depends first and foremost on a sound match between the student's motives and abilities and the demands of the assignments, responsibilities, and environments encountered. Piaget uses the concept of "optimal distance" to describe a good fit. Others talk about "readiness" and "preparation." I like the magnet and iron filings metaphor: If the distance between the filings and the magnet is too great, nothing happens. If the filings are close, they jump quickly but not far. But if the distance is just right, they can travel far—gradually at first, but with continuous acceleration. The maximum distance they cover is a function of the strength of the magnet, the weight of the filings, and the amount of friction. Experienced teachers know the pulling power of various books, writing assignments, and examination questions. Good teachers know how to make early judgments about which students are far away and which of them are on top of the subject matter. They can vary the distance accordingly and apply a little lubrication as needed.

Most of us, however, have had little experience matching students with experiential learning opportunities. It is a difficult task because the requirements are so complex. The range of fatal flaws is great and so are the opportunities for their expression. Different experiential alternatives offer different possibilities. Which do we want to exploit or emphasize? Would involvement in another culture or subculture be pertinent to our objectives? At what level? As a paid worker? A volunteer? A family member? An observer? Is practical work experience at the pre-, para-, or professional level appropriate? At what level of responsibility? With what degrees of freedom? And what seems to be the appropriate balance between career exploration or self-testing on the one hand and straightforward development of knowledge and competence on the other? Is analysis of organizational structure, behavioral norms, individual styles, and values useful? What about questions of social action and change? If we encourage systematic analyses, what do we do with the results? What do we do with critical reactions and creative recommendations that may arise whether we plan for them or not? If the activity is simply a field research project, what happens to the results? What educational values flow from sharing the results with subjects or potential target audiences?

Perhaps the most difficult questions arise when some important kinds of knowledge and competence called for in a given setting lie outside our own areas of understanding and expertise. I may be well schooled in the history of race relations, but I may understand little about the psychological dynamics of prejudice or about the mechanisms that lie behind perceptual selectivity and distortion. My grasp of the substantial research and theory in that area may not simply be limited; I may be totally ignorant of them. How, then, can I help students deal in sound academic fashion with such issues if they become integral to their research projects? I may feel completely incapacitated when it comes to dealing with outbursts of hostility or irrationality, or with curious logic based on blind spots or rigidities. Should I risk such eventualities for myself and for my students? I know that functioning effectively as a day care center aide and staff member will require high levels of interpersonal competence and sensitivity to group processes at work, both among the staff members and between them and the parents. I thoroughly understand small children, early childhood education curricula, and appropriate teaching activities; but can I help students develop the other skills and sensitivities necessary for successful functioning and a positive experience? Or will they get caught in political battles and personality conflicts that minimize other learning and turn their professional or intellectual interests elsewhere?

These questions are not really new. They sometimes come up in regular courses and seminars. But they arise with special force as we incorporate concrete experiences and active experimentation or application. The Early Childhood Education course addressed some of these questions quite explicitly. So did the Counseling Theory and Practice course and some of the related contracts.

The two key points are these: First, when we add significant dimensions of experiential learning to our accustomed array of reading, writing, assignments, or other tasks, we also may add areas of necessary competence and knowledge that stretch our limits or are, in fact, beyond our reach. Whether or not we wish to exploit these forces for learning, it is usually well to recognize them. If they are left unrecognized and undealt with, the colors they add create a confusing picture. Dealing with such areas responsibly requires additional learning on the part of faculty or additional resources to handle teaching and evaluation. Both are often required.

Second, we need thorough information about each setting, what it requires, what it can offer, what its resources are. And because settings can change with surprising speed, the information must be current. Who is going to obtain this information? Ideally, the faculty member most directly involved should have it firsthand from both the students and the agencies. Do faculty members have the necessary skills and understanding to obtain such information? Can they find the time? How much is lost if a third party obtains the information and supplies it? Should the third party do the matching? Will that party have sufficient understanding of the substantive content and desired competence to make sound judgments? How about a team? Fine. How many different faculty members in how many different areas can one "experiential learning professional" assist? Are we moving into another set of institutional support services with added costs and more bureaucratic arrangements? Perhaps.

Even with the best information at hand, we are sure to make errors. The consequences usually are minor disruptions and inconveniences, but occasionally they involve serious problems for the student, the cooperating agency or individual, and the educational institution. Who does the troubleshooting and maintains the working relationships? Who picks up the pieces when things come apart? Again, the responsible faculty member ought to handle these matters. But is there the competence, time, and energy?

The great temptation is to match students and settings in ways that maximize comfort and minimize problems. That strategy may leave everyone feeling happy and warm, but unfortunately it also may result in little learning. Optimal distance for learning requires a certain amount of mismatch. Most significant learning involves disequilibrium, upset, discontinuity, and differentiation before new levels of equilibrium and integration can be achieved. Thus, the whole matter of matching students and experiential opportunities remains a complex problem.

Efforts to deal with this problem lead to screening, selection, and orientation activities for both the students and the agencies. Depending upon the particular opportunities to be used, some students may be judged unready. What then? Are educational activities undertaken to help them? Are they precluded from study in certain areas? Do we end up running multiple tracks?

In addition, basic skills may be required that most students lack. Students may need training or practice in participant observation, or in simple reporting and description of events or activities uncolored by their own reactions and opinions. They may not know how to carry out an unstructured client-centered interview, or how to use a structured interview form in ways that obtain necessary information without constraining responses or creating frustration, anxiety, or contempt on the part of the interviewee. They may be unable to distinguish a log that keeps a time record of activities from a journal that expresses reactions, observations, opinions, and free associations. Does this kind of training become part of the course or should it be independent study? Is it best done separately for each class by each teacher? Is it handled generally for all students? Is credit granted for such learning?

Once students are under way, then problems of supervision, control, and ongoing evaluation arise. When teachers see students weekly in classes and have full responsibility for their work, they have a pretty strong sense of control—of their ability to monitor progress as it occurs and to deal with problems as they arise. They may be wrong in that assumption, but usually they feel comfortable with it nevertheless. When student contact is less frequent, when major activities are occurring elsewhere, when opportunities for personal intervention become limited, then teachers get nervous about whether conscientious work and learning are really going on. They may find logs, letters, journals, and the like helpful. Written reports, too, can be reassuring. But sometimes teachers are amazed at how heavily they lean on the crutch of class attendance. Somehow if students are showing up for class and seem interested, teachers think things are going along pretty well. Without that crutch they suddenly feel shaky. Confidence in the quality of supervision and evaluation provided by on-site personnel makes a big difference. Visits also can be helpful, but one wonders how much an artificial environment is created for the occasion. Dropping in unannounced often is inappropriate and disruptive.

These problems need to be solved, not simply to put the teacher more at ease but because effective ongoing evaluation is central to any learning program. Unless careful and systematic arrangements are made for self-evaluation by students and for external feedback and evaluation by others, learning will surely suffer. Evaluation plays an especially important role in situations where there is deep and intensive immersion in the experiences and with the other persons involved.

Often the evaluative activities themselves and the products generated for evaluation provide the only occasions for those critical steps of observation, reflection, and abstract conceptualization, which can lead to higher levels of active experimentation and application. Developing effective methods and criteria for evaluation is undoubtedly the most difficult part of any teaching program, and it certainly is the most challenging problem for experiential learning.

Summative evaluation, where allocating credits and credentials usually is involved, raises a different set of issues. How much credit do we grant for what kinds of learning, and under what kinds of conditions? For traditional practices, these basic issues have been buried by a pile of conventions. Our key convention is the typical formula that stipulates one hour of academic credit for one hour of class time plus two hours of preparation each week for about 15 weeks. In addition, there is the assumption that a typical three-credit course meets three times each week or once each week for three hours. From this basic framework, numerous wrinkles have been developed to accommodate laboratory work, intensive coursework, quarter systems, and shortened semesters. I assume there was logic in this formula when it was developed, a rationale for those particular divisions of hours and weeks and for the values assigned to them. But I can find no one today who is able to articulate that logic, even though curriculum committees and course designers worry mightily about varied kinds of equivalencies whenever a new offering or alternative is proposed.

The credit system has been useful in providing a common currency, but now the value of the unit fluctuates so widely from institution to institution and from one area of learning to another that the system teeters on the brink of bankruptcy. We confront that bankruptcy when we try to establish some basis for crediting experiential learning. We need some new coin of realm, but we are not likely to have it very soon.

Meanwhile, each of us works within this system, developing our own rough standards about how much reading and writing we can reasonably expect from students. Our individual standards are influenced by the unwritten and unspoken limits of our department or institution, and when we change locations we make adjustments accordingly, albeit gradually.

We all know that underneath these conventions the amount of work expected by different teachers, and the work and learning actually accomplished by students, varies greatly from person to person, department to department, institution to institution. Recent analyses of relationships between tests as predictors of college success and grade-point averages found that errors occurred chiefly because of high variability in grading practices rather than because the tests were invalid or unreliable. Curriculum planners also recognize that the meaning and worth of a degree vary widely—not only among institutions but also within the same institution. Institutional averages on Graduate Record Examination scores have been found to range from the tenth to the ninetieth percentile. The current emphasis on competency-based programs reflects concern about that variability and about questions of quality control, credentialing, and equity. We have come to admit that "time served" does not adequately represent learning, nor is it a sound basis for credentials. So we reach for better indices.

The problem with experiential learning is that there are as yet no conventions, guidelines, or even informal understandings that help an individual faculty member, a department, or an institution decide how much credit should be granted. Time served does not seem appropriate, given the number of hours most students invest and given the extreme variability in the educational value of activities pursued during those hours. But in the absence of any other framework or of any basic logic for our typical credit-hour system, we fly by the seat of our pants with whatever rationales and rationalizations we can develop for the particular case at hand. Having to work all of that out presents difficult problems of judgment. More importantly, perhaps, it leaves us feeling like a squirrel on a limb, an exposed target for those who sit secure and righteous on their couch of unexamined conventions and unarticulated assumptions.

Although being thus exposed may be more exhilarating than some of us would like, the decisions are probably more healthy and sound than the routine ones we usually run off in such uncritical fashion. They are sound precisely because of the more systematic attention given to the whole process. Those carefully considered judgments, made for particular kinds of students in a particular setting, trying to achieve defined purposes and evaluated on the basis of diverse evidence and methods, are probably some of the best we make. But that does not make the problem easier to solve, or make us more secure as we venture new judgments in a foreign territory.

These problems concerning purposes, substance, and quality are more or less significant, depending upon the experiential opportunities employed. The levels of responsibility and exposure involved in the Bioresearch and Race Relations courses are such that there is little need for detailed information about students and agencies or for complicated screening, selection, and orientation processes. There are no critical issues in matching students and alternatives. Neither are there problems concerning supervision, ongoing evaluation, credits to be awarded, and the like. The basic structure is provided by the content and the class meetings. Evaluation is based almost entirely on products and activities related to those contexts.

The Counseling Theory and Practice and the Early Childhood Education courses presented more substantial problems. In the Counseling course, students select a field experience from among different settings with clients who have quite different kinds of problems. Counseling and training mothers with newborn children will emphasize reassurance, information giving, training activities, helping clients deal with anxieties about new responsibilities, and shifting relationships with the father. Cases in which there are major emotional disturbances or substantial problems in personality structure probably will be infrequent. In contrast, counseling obese adolescents and their parents will typically engage the student with more deep-seated difficulties, with more emotionally loaded and intransigent parent-child dynamics. This setting will call for significantly more sophistication and self-understanding, clearer perspectives on one's own authority relationships, and a better grip on one's own values and assumptions.

A student who functions well in the first setting may be bowled over in the second. In either case, good supervision and sound relationships between students and the cooperating agencies are essential. The limits of student responsibility and appropriate actions when difficulties arise must be clearly understood. Ongoing evaluation must be guaranteed. Both the teacher and the agency will want to screen and orient students and will want to be able to remove those who are creating problems for the clients, for themselves, or for the agency. The same conditions obtain with somewhat less force for the day care center aides. In this case, the range of responsibilities a particular student may assume and the flexibility of the setting provide greater chances to capitalize on strengths and to minimize the negative consequences of weaknesses, even as a student works to remedy them.

Individual learning contracts are useful devices for experiential learning, largely because many of the problematic judgments concerning purposes, substance, and quality can be made with greater confidence for a single person than for a group. We can obtain detailed information concerning prior experiences. New experiential opportunities can be tested on a trial basis and the range of responsibilities can be increased as both student and agency recognize possibilities and find ways to use them. Arrangements for personal contact, supervision, and ongoing evaluation can be tight or relaxed, as dictated by the needs of the student and teacher, by the kinds of learning under way, and by the setting. Judgments concerning the credit to be granted can rest on detailed information about the activities pursued, the time and energy invested, and the apparent outcomes. Those judgments can be posited at the outset and can be modified up or down as the learning contract proceeds and when a final decision is necessary. Faculty members are relatively secure in the decisions they make because their rich knowledge of the students and the learning accomplished greatly exceeds that of any outside persons. If the faculty member functions responsibly, substantive challenges can be answered with reason and information.

The problem, of course, is that the values of individualized contracts also confront us with the significance of individual differences and their consequences for learning. To respond to these differences, we recognize the need for more diverse settings and more diverse levels of challenge within them. Thus we become caught in a cycle of infinitely expanding complexity and a geometrically expanding workload. Then the temptation is to say, "Oh, the heck with it. I can't manage all this. Let's just stick with lectures and discussions, readings and writings. It's easier on all of us, and there's not much payoff for all this added effort anyway."

In similar fashion, as a typical course moves toward greater use of experiential components, there also develop pressures for greater individualization of purposes, substance, and expectations concerning outcomes. Because we are pushed to think more thoroughly about the students—where they are when they begin and what they will learn—and because we may have to worry about screening and orientation, we recognize individual differences more explicitly and try to respond so that each student makes maximum progress. These efforts generate the need for additional resources and assistance to deal with the increased workload and the range of responsibilities that lie outside the interest or competence of most faculty members. Thus, problems of educational quality at the level of faculty members and their students become problems of institutional support, as well as of staffing, budget, organization, and community relations.

4

Problems: Institutional Support

SIGNIFICANT INSTITUTIONAL RESOURCES ARE NECESSARY if faculty members and students across a wide range of disciplinary, interdisciplinary, professional, and vocational studies are to undertake experiential learning. Consider what will be necessary if the kinds of concrete experiences and opportunities for application and active experimentation illustrated by the courses and contracts in this book were expanded throughout the curriculum. When an occasional faculty member is developing such activities and when only a few students are involved, it may be sufficient to leave matters entirely to their own initiative and completely in their hands. But if substantial numbers of faculty begin to do likewise, then coordination among them and planning for measured use of available opportunities is required. Otherwise, cooperating agencies receive conflicting and overlapping requests and may find themselves pressured to do more than they can or wish to do. Furthermore, if the institution aims to encourage such activities by faculty members and students, and if it wants to avoid the faculty reactions that set in when individual initiative, time, and energy go unrecognized, then supporting staff and budget allocations are required.

There is nothing surprising or unique about the need for institutional support. Few institutions would presume to operate without at least minimum library collections pertinent to major areas of study, managed by a staff that makes them accessible and keeps them up-to-date. A college would not expect laboratory sciences to be pursued without providing facilities on campus or access to them elsewhere, with appropriate maintenance personnel and laboratory assistants. Similarly, if students and faculty are to make significant use of experiential learning, a "library" of opportunities, a support staff, and additional resources for adequate information and access will be required.

Clearly, it will not be possible financially to begin full-blown with the total range of opportunities eventually desired, nor would it be sound to do so. The way to proceed is not much different from the typical way library collections are built—through active consultation with faculty members, department chairmen, division heads, and the like, and in response to special requests from individuals. As often happens with books, a beginning usually can be made simply by soliciting contributions from students and faculty members concerning settings they have used or likely resource possibilities with which they are familiar.

The most critical necessity at the outset is a full-time professional whose primary responsibility is helping faculty members locate and use effectively varied settings and resource persons for concrete experiences and active application or experimentation. This first professional should be both a peer and a colleague, with full faculty status. If he or she does not have a track record as an effective teacher and scholar at the institution, then the job description should call for such activities. To be most effective, this person will not simply be running errands, making contacts, and doing leg work. The key requirement for success essentially involves being a teacher to the faculty, helping them understand the contributions of varied opportunities for direct experiences, helping them learn how to integrate such activities with their accustomed expectations concerning reading, writing, examinations, and the like. If this professional cannot help faculty members pursue their own development with regard to the changes in teaching practices required, then only halting progress will occur. In my judgment, most attempts to introduce and expand activities of experiential learning fail because junior persons are employed who lack the experience and maturity necessary to establish collegial relationships of mutual respect with a wide range of faculty members. Such maturity is no less important in the field, where the ability to deal effectively with agency directors, corporate executives, and others is equally critical.

This first requirement for institutional resources presents a set of problems that are not always easily solved. Finding the dollars to support a high-level position is difficult. It may be even more difficult to give the position sufficient stature within the institution to be attractive either to a respected faculty member, an administrator already employed, or to a newly hired person with the appropriate background. Someone is needed who will make a fairly long-term commitment and who has a strong investment in building a solid program. But this profession is still new, without a clearly identified career pattern or reward system. It is hard to build anything well by relying solely on persons who will take responsibility for a year or two and then return to a more attractive home base. In this effort, continuity is especially important where so much depends upon well-nurtured working relationships with cooperating individuals and agencies. High turnover, even when it is handled conscientiously by those who leave, is a handicap. Thus it is important to attract a senior person who will make a substantial commitment and stick with it, whatever the hurdles.

Another critical institutional resource is time and energy from top administrators: the president, the academic vice president, the executive vice president. When a program is getting under way, active support from these persons will be essential. Aside from internal support, these contributions primarily take the form of meetings with executives of large enterprises that offer diverse possibilities: hospital directors, corporation presidents, school superintendents, health commissioners, civil service directors at all levels of government, museum directors, and so on. Clear understanding from the top eases subordinates' anxieties and smooths the way for more detailed negotiations. Once initial agreements have been established, working relationships can be maintained by the responsible professional—unless severe difficulties arise. These appointments are not likely to consume major periods of time in any given week or month; an average of one or two contacts per week is probably the maximum. But such expenditure of time will be necessary, at least during the first year or two.

The third critical element is support from the system: approval and encouragement from the academic policy committee, curriculum committee, or other appropriate faculty governance bodies. In many institutions such approval will not be required before starting a program. Usually there are ways to proceed without creating explicit challenges to such groups. But if substantial institutionwide efforts are to mature, courses and alternative programs will be developed that require approval. Therefore it is important to begin cultivating the soil early: find resources for key faculty members so they experience positive rewards; provide periodic reports, testimonials, and hard evidence; meet informally with appropriate groups to deal with questions; work collaboratively to assure that sound standards are maintained.

If these three elements—an experienced, competent professional, active support at the top, and system approval—are in place, then the basis will have been laid for other key ingredients. These will include not only adequate secretarial services and travel money but also vehicles or transportation services, where necessary, so students can reach available opportunities. As the program develops, qualified junior personnel will be necessary to troubleshoot for the director and to help maintain communications with the diverse faculty, students, and agencies involved. However, none of these will be required if the three key elements are not firmly in place.

Achieving broad-based institutional support means dealing with institutional resistance to change and innovation. "Resistance" means "to withstand, to be proof against, to be able to repel, as a disease." It is a two-way street. Often the difficulty in getting a new idea accepted lies more with the characteristics of those bitten by the bug of innovation than with the bug itself. Carriers of experiential learning often suffer from one of two diseases—and sometimes from both. There are those who suffer from—to borrow Ewald Nyquist's delightful phrase—The Impotence of Being Earnest, and there are—to distort Dewey's label—the Either/Orneries.

True believers, of course, are necessary to any significant social change, but many persons simply dig in their heels when they are confronted with new notions. Such reactions are particularly common among academic intellectuals who prize dispassionate rationality, cool debate, and carefully balanced pros and cons. The Either/Orneries may actually be advanced cases of The Impotence of Being Earnest. They not only require that you see the light and take the new path, but that you cast out all prior beliefs and behaviors. They do not simply neglect the contributions of traditional practices and the complexities of effective integration; they reject them. In that rejection, they foster hostility and create active resistance where openness, thoughtful consideration, and measured change might otherwise have prevailed.

Such persons not only fuel and fan the flames of institutional resistance; they also contribute to a more fundamental problem: oversimplification and superficial thinking about teaching, learning, and education. Dewey argued strongly against these tendencies:

> The general principles of the new education do not of themselves solve any of the problems of the actual or practical conduct and management of progressive schools. Rather, they set new problems which have to be worked out on the basis of a new philosophy of experience. The problems are not even recognized, to say nothing of being solved, when it is assumed that it suffices to reject the ideas and practices of the old education and then go to the opposite extreme. Yet I am sure that you will appreciate what is meant when I say that many of the newer schools tend to make little or nothing of organized subject matter...to proceed as if any form of direction and guidance by adults were an invasion of individual freedom, and as if the idea that education should be concerned with the present and future meant that acquaintance with the past has little or no role to play....
>
> Without pressing these defects to the point of exaggeration, they at least illustrate what is meant by a theory and practice of education which proceeds negatively or by reaction against what has been current...rather than by a positive and constructive development of purposes, methods, and subject matter on the foundation of a theory of experience and its educational potentialities.
>
> It is not too much to say that an educational philosophy which professes to be based on the idea of freedom may become as dogmatic as ever was the traditional education which is reacted against. For any theory and set of practices is dogmatic which is not based upon critical examination of its own underlying principles. [7]

The following comparative lists illustrate a mild form of Either/Orneriness:

Meta Goals of Traditional College and University Classrooms	Appropriate Meta Goals for Cross-Cultural Training
Source of Information: Information comes from experts and authoritative sources through the media of books, lectures, audiovisual presentations. "If you have a question look it up."	Source of Information: Information sources must be developed by learner from the social environment. Information gathering methods include observation and questioning of associates, other learners, and chance acquaintances.
Learning Settings: Learning takes place in settings designated for the purpose, e.g., classrooms and libraries.	Learning Settings: The entire social environment is the setting for learning. Every human encounter provides relevant information.
Problem-Solving Approaches: Problems are defined and posed to the learner by experts and authorities. The correct problem-solving methods are specified, and the student's work is checked for application of the proper method and for accuracy, or at least for reasonableness of results. The emphasis is on solutions to known problems.	Problem-Solving Approaches: The learner is on his own to define problems, generate hypotheses, and collect information from the social environment. The emphasis is on discovering problems and developing problem-solving approaches on the spot.

7. Dewey, *Experience and Education*, pp. 21-22.

Meta Goals of Traditional College and University Classrooms	Appropriate Meta Goals for Cross-Cultural Training
Role of Emotions and Values: Problems are largely dealt with at an ideational level. Questions of reason and of fact are paramount. Feelings and values may be discussed but are rarely acted upon.	*Role of Emotions and Values:* Problems are usually value- and emotion-laden. Facts are often less relevant than the perceptions and attitudes which people hold. Values and feelings have action consequences, and action must be taken.
Criteria of Successful Learning: Favorable evaluation by experts and authorities of the quality of the individual's intellectual productions, primarily written work.	*Criteria of Successful Learning:* The establishment and maintenance of effective and satisfying relationships with others in the work setting. This includes the ability to communicate with and influence others. Often there are no criteria available other than the attitudes of the parties involved in the relationship.[8]

There is nothing violently wrong with these juxtapositions and assertions. Indeed, there is a good bit of truth in most of them. But they are exaggerated enough to leave skewed impressions. I know of many classes where the students and not the teacher pose the problems and the emphasis is on original solutions to new issues— and classes where questions of value are raised directly by the readings and in the discussions. Not every human encounter provides relevant information, nor does the learner always strictly define his problems or solve them. Faculty and administrators are fundamentally correct in rejecting the importunings of the earnest and the attacks of the Either/Orneries. Although the direction they point to may be sound, their approach will not lead us toward more effective education.

Effective change occurs by moving toward and working with others, not by creating polar extremes. It's not very different from effective teaching. The needs and values of others have to be recognized and taken into account. The optimal distance between the innovation and those who need to change must be found. Basically, the process of mutual adaptation should be such that as the institution and interested faculty members move toward innovation, so also the innovation moves toward the institution. Conditions have to be created so that joint movement can occur through discussion, compromise, negotiation, self-examination, and development.

Of course, most persons concerned with experiential education do not approximate the caricatures of the earnest or ornery. Most advocates of change are thoughtful and analytic concerning current educational practices; they have actively experimented themselves, testing their ideas in practice, reaching for creative modifications that add new muscle to traditional practices and purposes. They proceed deliberately, sensitively, and with respect for the views and experiences of others. Yet, change reaches the level of faculty teaching behavior very slowly indeed.

There are fundamental reasons why faculty change comes slowly. Even the most effective strategies will not quickly alter the underlying realities. First, a lot of work is involved. Redefining purposes,

8. R. Harrison and R. Hopkins, "The Design of Cross-Cultural Training: An Alternative to the University Model," *Journal of Applied Behavioral Science* (1967), Vol. 3, No. 4, pp. 437-438.

revising reading lists, devising new assignments, rewriting examinations, and creating additional methods of evaluation are not only challenging but also time-consuming tasks. They are burdens added to busy schedules, seldom supported by released time or contexts where collegial support, suggestions, and constructive criticism are available. Second, new teaching arrangements may disrupt comfortable routines and leave us less in control of our own schedules. Meetings at unaccustomed hours during evenings or weekends may be necessary. Interruptions from phone calls and visitors may escalate. Boring and routine correspondence may increase. We may have to fuss with small budget items. We may find ourselves dealing with more and more administrative detail. Is it worth the cost?

Third, basic stylistic preferences and teaching orientations may be threatened. I may depend on the privacy, quiet, and protection of my study, my books, my lecture notes. Meeting my classes and dealing with a few especially curious or energetic students may be all the outreach I want. Or I may genuinely enjoy performing before a group, getting students' attention and holding it, creating enthusiasm where only mild interest existed before. The role of expert may be deeply satisfying. Preparing thoroughly and maintaining strict control may provide security, recognition, and a sense of achievement very hard to relinquish. Why should I get to know practitioners and spend time talking about their problems? Why should I encourage a situation in which students may introduce new considerations that simply distract me and the class from the theoretical complexities that are so satisfying and worthwhile? These concrete experiences and practical applications may be well and good and may eventually be necessary—but not now, not for my students, not for me to deal with.

A fourth reason faculty change comes slowly is the complex of uncertainties concerning standards and quality. How can I be sure my students will learn as much as they did in the past when time formerly spent on substantial readings and writings now goes into direct experiences, observations, and reflections? How can we cover the same amount of ground if I introduce activities that require application and experimentation? How will I cope if these experiential elements get students excited about some tangent that deflects us from our purposes and disrupts my carefully constructed sequence and relationships, evolved through several semesters of this course?

Perhaps the most significant forces of resistance lie in latent or explicit concerns about competence and significance. Do I have the competence to work with students in this new way? Can I function well when external agencies and supervisors are influencing the course of student learning, the substance of my teaching, the nature of my relationships with students? Can I meet practitioners on their own grounds and understand the difficulties of their work? Or will I seem naive, cloistered, ineffectual, unrealistic? And what if practitioners, and then my students, find the information, insights, research, and theories irrelevant, erroneous, contrary to their experiences? What then? Where am I left with regard to the meaning and value of my teaching and scholarship?

I do not believe these are fanciful questions, or that they exist only for an insecure and insignificant minority of teachers. I believe they exist for experienced, successful teachers as well as for the young and inexperienced. They exist widely because they are, in fact, real. The concerns and the issues raised often turn out to be justified. Making changes often involves hard work and inconvenience. It may call for elaborating additional styles and for substantial shifts in teaching orientation. It may sometimes turn out that we not only "cover less ground," but that student learning is less thorough and less useful. Many of us will not have the ready-made understanding and competence to work effectively with practitioners, to understand their environments and needs. Furthermore, our information, insights, research, and theories certainly will prove wanting even if they are not erroneous.

Wishing to change slowly seems to me completely understandable. Moreover, it is basically sound, because in order to achieve such changes each of us will have to take Coleman's steps and go through Kolb's experiential learning cycle not once but many times as we test our new ideas in action, experience the consequences, reflect on those experiences, and develop new ideas for further testing. To think otherwise would be to assume some magic by which learning and personal development occur for faculty members and administrators that is different from the way in which we assume they occur for students. So far there exists little evidence for such magic.

Institutional change is needed to create the conditions where experiential learning by faculty members can occur; where they can deal with questions concerning competence, coverage, convenience; where there are resources and rewards that support the added work necessary to take new steps. But if institutional change requires action by faculty committees and a senate, then each of those governance units becomes a forum for the full range of anxieties and questions we have discussed—and for many more that will occur to creative academics with sharply honed critical skills. Calls for cautious deliberation will echo across the campus. The following letter to the editor of a college newspaper is an archetype:

> Your editorial "Can Our Faculty Learn?" raises an intriguing question. I want to assure you and your readers that we can learn and, in fact, have learned much. Our vote on the proposal for...experiential learning was based not on ignorance (as you seem to suggest) but on experience.... Like faculties all over the country, we have learned a lot about how not to make decisions and, I hope, a few things about how to make good ones. Faculties know that it is not sensible to say yes quickly, just because some colleagues have spent a good deal of time and thought on the subject. They know from experience that complicated matters like experiential learning take much thought and discussion; that it is essential that some of this discussion take place in relatively small groups where a good deal of give-and-take is possible. Our vote last week was not intended to give us time to simply stand by and wait to be educated. Sensible decisions by a group require time for the study of the proposal in detail; for sorting out varying points of view; for estimating how much, if any, of the proposal is acceptable; for drafting regulations which embody an acceptable policy; and, finally, for debating and voting. All this takes a great deal of time and energy, but faculties are eager to invest time and energy for the sake of sensible decisions on important questions.

That letter rings all the bells heard so often when change is proposed. Despite the fact that colleagues have given it a "good deal of time and thought," much more thought and discussion are required. Look at all the details of the program. Pick it apart to see whether any small piece might be acceptable. Then see what changes in regulations and policies might be required. Formulate those and examine them. Then, if it is not already dead of old age or unrecognizable, subject the proposed change to further debate and perhaps to a vote. There is one thing on which the author of the letter and I agree. It certainly does seem true that many faculties are eager to invest time and energy in such activities.

It is not so much the substance of such a letter that is discouraging; it is the spirit and assumptions that lie behind it. Obviously, any substantial proposal deserves careful thought—but must our reflex assumptions be that it is flawed; that only some small portion will be acceptable; that the substantial time and thought of our colleagues have produced recommendations of only limited merit? The author puts his orientation well when he indicates that he and his colleagues have learned a lot about how not to make decisions and a few things about making good ones.

The letter also is significant for what it does not say. Anxieties concerning whether students will continue to enroll heavily in my courses or in our department are not articulated. There is no mention of the shifts in status, power, and security that may occur if institutional policies create possibilities for experiential learning. We can be sure that the issues of quality and substance will be thoroughly debated and openly attacked. We also can be sure that student enrollment, departmental status, individual security, and recognition are powerful concerns that will probably remain hidden in the debates—just as they have in the letter.

There are two ways to deal with the problem of collective faculty resistance through governance mechanisms: tackle it head-on or go one step at a time. Tackling it head-on means confronting a very complex range of issues, issues that move quickly to levels of abstraction that may challenge basic institutional purposes and policies. For precisely this reason the head-on approach can be extremely useful and healthy, assuming solid attention to substantive issues and minimal contamination by politics of status, income, and security. But while the faculty is investing two or three years in the necessary debate and redefinition, not much is apt to happen to teaching and learning. However, the process may conclude with a major commitment to substantial change, adequate funding, a reasonably broad base of support, and a congenial environment.

That kind of planned change is complex. It requires not only dedicated leadership but also competent persons who are knowledgeable about organizational behavior, who understand the processes by which change occurs, and who are experienced in helping it happen. There is a lot of literature in this area, but unfortunately most of it does not focus on higher education. The major exception is Jack Lindquist's new book, *Strategies for Change: Innovation as Adaptive Development* (Pacific Soundings Press, San Diego). Based on action research concerning curricular change at eight institutions, it presents an original synthesis of preexisting formulations, some detailed case studies, and general propositions useful to anyone tackling problems of institutional change.

The other way to change is to go one step at a time. Few faculty members, administrators, or committees have the temerity to question a colleague's judgment concerning choice of subject matter and

teaching methods. Much poor teaching persists because of that re-
luctance, but it also makes possible substantial innovation by individuals and departments. The most effective approach may be an
incremental one that begins by helping interested faculty expand
the range of settings they use and the subjects for which experiential learning is judged pertinent. At least the changes are occurring
where they count—in the actual behavior of faculty members and
students—and not simply at the level of institutional rhetoric and
general policy statements. Moreover, interested persons are chang-
ing their own behavior; they are showing and not just telling; they
are backing up word with deed.

Such incremental change often works with surprising speed when
early ventures yield clear and immediate benefits. As the
range of experienced persons grows, their influence grows even
faster. Good ideas demonstrated in practice and accompanied by
some systematic efforts at exposure are often quickly adapted. The
critical point is to share and make public these early efforts.

The Keller plan and other adaptations under the PSI (Personalized
System of Instruction) rubric are a good example. At most institutions, the typical pattern of change has been incremental. An interested teacher comes upon an idea through a friend, in a journal, or
at a professional meeting. Materials developed by others and reports of their experiences with typical courses come to light. A new
idea seems worth trying, and materials are adopted unaltered or
adapted to fit local needs. The experience seems to work out well.
Students report that they find it a good way to learn. Their test
scores equal or surpass those of other students in traditional sections. Teacher time and energy can be transferred from information
giving and testing to troubleshooting and more complex work with
students. Other teachers in the department or division pick up the
idea, and the first teacher begins to develop original materials for a
different course. No major policy issues are confronted; no governance mechanisms are called into play. The faculty simply modifies
its teaching in ways that offer increased success and satisfaction.

Though the process is complex because it extends beyond the
teacher and the immediate classroom or laboratory, improved
teaching through increased use of experiential learning can be managed. If significant discontinuities vis-à-vis traditional institutional
purposes or educational principles occur when change becomes
widespread, they can be dealt with. Under those conditions, issues
will be resolved on a reasonably broad basis of experience, observation, abstract conceptualization, and active experimentation.
Sufficient faculty members will have learned enough to make well-
considered judgments, undistorted by the ambiguities and anxieties
that flow from partial knowledge and limited experience.

Of course, institutional resistance also can be largely due to limited dollars and tough priorities. When faculty positions and support services are static or must be cut, adding a professional position and supporting funds to encourage experiential learning may
be out of the question. Even if soft money can be found to support
start-up costs for two or three years, long-term commitment to hard-
money support may be not only injudicious but irresponsible as well.
Under these conditions, one step at a time, achieved by small reallo-
cations of responsibilities for interested faculty members and ad-

ministrators, may be the only alternative. If these changes can be supplemented with workshops, seminars, and various kinds of professional and institutional development projects, change toward increased use of experiential learning may be accelerated. Once such sufficient groundwork has been accomplished, a boom or a bust may provide occasion either for budgetary additions for more staff and support or for retrenchment and reorganization.

Today there is no broad base of scientific data and research that focuses directly on the evaluation of experiential learning programs. We must therefore rely on empirical data from persons and institutions that have developed and carried out various kinds of programs. This experience is of long duration in a few institutions and is accumulating rapidly in many others. Publications and conferences are beginning to emerge. An institution interested in making changes can probably find another college or university with similar experience, and the twice-yearly meetings of CAEL assembly institutions make wide consultation and exchange more easily accessible.

However, the absence of broad-based research continues. We need multi-institutional studies, undertaken with the best scientific rigor we can currently muster in the behavioral sciences. We also need tough-minded studies undertaken by individual institutions. Until such a solid foundation of research and evaluation is created, it will be hard to make systematic progress with the tough issues concerning purposes, substance, and quality.

5

Potentials for Students
and Educational Effectiveness

DOES EXPERIENTIAL LEARNING HOLD ENOUGH PROMISE TO offset the diverse problems posed by defining purposes, substance, and quality? With current budgetary constraints and endemic difficulties in carrying forward institutional development, which affects teaching and learning, are there sufficient potential benefits to justify introducing such activities or extending current efforts throughout the curriculum? What are some of the payoffs that may result if academics invest the time, energy, and dollars required to take significant steps in the direction of change?

Each college and university will have to answer these questions in terms of its particular mission, its current status, its needs, and its sense of effectiveness. The experiential mode carries significant potentials for students, faculty members, and institutions to warrant serious consideration. But we cannot suggest how the actual trade-offs might emerge after they are weighed by a particular faculty and administration.

Consider first the potentials for student learning. Probably the most important factor here is motivation. An apprentice, intern, or aide who is carrying responsibilities in a professional or vocational area regularly discovers gaps in competence or knowledge. A volunteer helping a community agency sees ways in which further learning could lead to more substantial service. A concerned citizen actively tackling a social problem discovers some complex issues requiring insights from several disciplines. When such activities become part of college studies, clarity of purpose and strength of motivation are enhanced and sustained by the momentum of the ongoing responsibilities. The rewards that come from bringing order to experience through reflection and abstract conceptualization, the excitement of seeing knowledge and skills effectively applied, the sense of making real gains in working knowledge create a self-amplifying process that generates increased energy and commitment for further learning.

It is probably no coincidence that the growing interest in experiential learning has occurred during a time when the percentage of adult and part-time students has increased sharply and when open access has increased enrollments of students whose prior learning has not been bookish or academic. The primary motivations of such students usually relate to some immediate interest or to the desire to handle a job, a family, or a community responsibility more effectively. These students do not typically start out interested in ideas for the sheer pleasure of intellectual pursuit. Learning linked to pragmatic concerns and present realities provides a better grip on daily existence; that, in turn, can create the perspective and space for more general studies.

These persons have typically learned by starting with experience and then trying to make sense of it so they might function better. They have not typically started with the observations, reflections, or abstract concepts of others and then gone looking for experiential illustrations. Thus, both the motives and the learning styles of these new students—who have rapidly come to outnumber the traditional middle- and upper-middle-class intellectuals of the past—create a strong force for effective integration of experience and education.

These students are not likely to diminish in number or in their interest in higher education. Successful learning tends to beget a desire for more learning. Lifelong learning will increasingly become a reality for many persons, not only because social changes and multiple careers create the need for new knowledge, skills, and perspectives but also because learning itself provides intrinsic satisfactions for many. Once these satisfactions are tasted, most people go back for additional helpings to feed their growing interests and social consciousness. Thus the number of mature persons coming to college rich in experience will increase much faster than the number of young persons who are rich only in prior schooling. Demands that the rich experiences of adulthood be recognized and incorporated into ongoing educational activities will become more insistent.

With solid motivation fueling active participation, the chance for more substantial and complex learning increases. Higher level intellectual skills of application, analysis, synthesis, and evaluation may be fostered when solving complex problems requires more than rote memory or simple recall of facts and figures. Those students who work in various counseling settings will not serve their clients well by offering up simple textbook homilies or by adopting stilted postures and phrases from one or another counseling theorist. The day care center aides can function as helpful staff only if they examine innovative practices elsewhere and make recommendations that integrate information and experiences from diverse sources, analyze relationships among programs and activities, and evaluate the strengths and weaknesses of various alternatives. The individuals pursuing environmental and American studies will need to use wide-ranging skills of observation, analysis, synthesis, and evaluation to bring some order to the multitude of readings, persons, and environments they encounter.

The active engagement with social issues and human problems provided by many experiential learning opportunities also encourages what Robert W. White calls "the development of humanitarian concern" and what Alfred Adler earlier called "the development of social interest." These writers are talking about the capacity to invest oneself in concerns beyond one's immediate self-interest and personal gain, the capacity to identify oneself with the welfare of others. Gordon Allport said, "Maturity advances in proportion as lives are decentered from the clamorous immediacy of body and ego-centeredness. Self-love is a prominent and inescapable factor in every life but it need not dominate. Everybody has self-love, but only self-extension is the earmark of maturity." [9] When students encounter the human consequences of pollution and racial discrimination, when they see the shortfall in human services delivery systems and in criminal justice, when experiences of social stratification are projected against the rhetoric of democracy, then the foundations for more enlightened citizenship and more active contribution are strengthened.

In addition to strengthening motivation, fostering more complex intellectual skills, and strengthening perspectives for effective citizenship, experiential learning also can speak to our increasing concerns about accountability and the general contributions made by higher education. Sharp questions are being asked about the "value added" principle beyond that already determined by parents' occupation, income, and schooling and by the student's educational achievement prior to college. Although colleges seem to serve a screening and credentialing function, we are uncertain about how much useful learning actually occurs. Studies of grade-point averages and postcollege achievement find little evidence of significant relationships. David McClelland's 1973 review of the literature is consistent with Hoyt's 1965 survey. McClelland says:

> Researchers have in fact had great difficulty demonstrating that grades in school are related to any other behaviors of importance.... Yet the general public—including many psychologists and most college officials—simply has been unable to believe or accept this fact. It seems so self-evident to educators that those who do well in their classes *must* go on to do better in life that they systematically have disregarded evidence to the contrary that has been accumulating for some time...being a high school or college graduate gave one a credential that opened up certain higher level jobs, but the poorer students in high school or college did as well in life as the top students...neither amount of education nor grades in school is related to vocational success as a factory worker, bank teller, or air traffic controller. Even for highly intellectual jobs like scientific researcher, superior on-the-job performance is related in no way to better grades in college. [10]

These consistent research findings suggest that our suspicions concerning the contributions of college may be well founded. Concerns about accountability and effectiveness have been escalating rapidly since the early 1970s when McClelland wrote these lines. Recent emphases on competency-based education and certification testify to concerns about the quality of working knowledge provided by traditional higher education. To some persons, it appears that integrated use of concrete experience and active application hold promise for improving the quality and usefulness of postsecondary

9. G.W. Allport, *Pattern and Growth in Personality* (New York: Holt, Rinehart & Winston, 1961), p. 165.
10. D.C. McClelland, "Testing for Competence Rather Than for 'Intelligence,'" *The American Psychologist* 28 (1973), p. 2.

education, and that this can help meet the increasing demands for lifelong learning.

One of the principal ways learning improves is by strengthening the links between ideas and the realities they refer to. Learning depends on two things: the ability to symbolize abstractly the events and objects of one's experience, and firsthand encounters with events and objects that give meaning to the inexact and abstract symbolic representations. When ideas are translated into specific acts, when theories concerning practice are realized through concrete behaviors, when abstract relationships are turned into tangible, visible products, then a strong and integrated system results that can be carried forward through time. If objects are not bound to symbols by action, they tend to remain fragmented and incoherent; if symbols are detached from reality, they remain hollow and limited. The "ivory tower," the "absentminded professor," and the walled-in university all reflect that detachment. It is a necessary but insufficient part of the learning process that becomes counterproductive when carried to extremes. In some cases we have almost mimicked the scholarly professor who, given a choice between going to paradise or going to a lecture about paradise, chose the latter. Most of us have met young professionals fresh from graduate training who are full of new information, keen insights, and original theoretical constructs. But we also recognize the lack of seasoning behind their brilliance. One sharp question from an experienced colleague and, like a punctured balloon, they collapse in a rush of hot air.

Strong links between ideas and realities, between rich experiences and conceptual organizers, increase retention. Information, principles, varied applications, knowledge of strengths and weaknesses remain available into the future. The knowledge and competence acquired by those day care center aides will not evaporate after the final examination; the understanding of alternative energy sources and of their potentialities and limitations, acquired from the travels and readings of that environmental studies student, will not have disappeared by the time he wants to build his own house, start a business, or undertake graduate studies in architecture, engineering, or ecology. Particulars may fade, as with any learning not regularly used, but a fast recovery system will have been created.

Another major contribution to the quality of learning is more general, but perhaps more fundamental. It occurs when students recognize that words in print are not absolute truths but are, instead, one person's particular organization of reality. Conversely, it occurs when students recognize that experience alone can be a poor and misleading teacher and that seeing can be deceiving, a distorted basis for belief. When students recognize that truth can only be approximated, that wisdom rests on multiple experiences perceived from diverse angles in varying lights and refracted through prisms of varying shape and composition, then the cornerstone for solid, active, and continued learning has been set. Then ideas will be held with more tenuous tenacity and actions taken with more openness and humility. Then the experiential learning cycle may become integrated into daily existence, making learning part of living rather than apart from it, to be pursued only in and for some institution or credential. Experiential learning also can lead to more effective integration between professional/vocational training and general or liberal education. Paul Barton puts the problem well:

> Too many Americans find themselves at two times in their lives in situations that almost perversely mirror each other. In the first, a young person just out of school or college pounds the pavements looking for a job, carrying the diploma by which the educational system certifies that one is prepared for adulthood. The first several employers that the graduate approaches quickly dismiss that particular meaning of a diploma. They say one must have experience in order to get a job. How does one get that experience? They do not say.
>
> In the second situation, an adult already well experienced at work, but without advanced education, wants further educational opportunity or an educational credential. But the currency of experience, in such short supply during youth, is not legal tender in the educational community; and the educational system requirements, schedules, and financing provisions seem forbiddingly out of step with the reality of adult life. It is widely said that experience is the best teacher. Scholars have said it too, although, of course, in many more words. But few give credit for its teaching.
>
> People seem to be able to move smoothly within the system of education, and within the system of experience, but not between them. For three quarters of a century, the linking mechanisms enabling one to move from high school to college and from one college to another have been honed through College Board scores, semester credit hours, standardized grading systems, and comparable transcripts. At the same time, employers generally have recognized the preparation given by other employers; and if there was any doubt about how well the prospective employee performed before, the answer was there for the asking. But connections remain inadequate at the crossovers between education and employment and between employment and education.[11]

Experiential learning can help establish crossovers between the academy and the world of work. It can provide young persons with pertinent experiences to accompany their diplomas. The simple fact of sound performance on a job is often more important than the extent to which experiences are directly related to the particular kinds of employment sought. One of the main reasons employers shy away from young persons is that they are skeptical of their stability, conscientiousness, and willingness to conform to the requirements of responsible functioning as subordinates. They question whether an unseasoned youth will recognize the importance of being on time, meeting deadlines and production targets, taking directions and acquiescing to authority, working harmoniously with others, and exercising initiative judiciously. Once a young person has demonstrated these capacities in one job, future prospects markedly improve—especially if there has been clear evidence of ability to learn quickly the requirements of particular situations. Experiential learning, therefore, can have practical payoffs for young persons competing for jobs in a tight market.

There is also a payoff in competition for graduate school admission. Graduate admissions officers and faculty members in programs that train students for particular professions—law, medicine, social work, and the like—rightly recognize that applicants who have had actual work or volunteer experiences related to their professional plans are better risks than those who have not. Experienced applicants have had a chance to test their interests and aspirations, to see what the work really involves on a day-to-day basis,

---

11. P. Barton, "Learning Through Work and Education," in Keeton, *Experiential Learning*, pp. 119, 120.

to understand the ratio of boredom and drudgery to excitement and romance, to put considerations of income and prestige in the perspective of emotional demands, time constraints, workload requirements, and other concrete realities. Those applicants also have a basis for understanding why various kinds of knowledge and competence are required and what their contributions can be. This does not always imply ready acceptance of institutional expectations; they may be perceived as outdated, irrelevant, or superficial. But it does mean that such students will bring motivation, curiosity, and a certain tough-mindedness that may often be lacking in applicants whose prior knowledge and competence come solely from books, lectures, and class discussions. The statistics for Antioch graduates, for example, show high rates of acceptance in graduate schools, not only because the students are bright and well prepared academically but also because most of them have had substantial work experiences in allied areas undertaken as part of their co-op work term or as an integrated part of their regular studies.

The crossover possibilities can be especially rich for older persons whose ongoing activities include varied responsibilities not only on the job but also at home, with the family, and in the community. Often these responsibilities, the environments in which they are pursued, the relationships involved, and the diverse persons encountered can themselves be resources for learning. They offer events and activities for observation and reflection, settings for application and active experimentation. Use of those built-in resources gives immediacy to academic learning and provides continued opportunity for relearning and reexamination. There are also the practical advantages of ready access, established working relationships, and convenience that often make it possible for adults to pursue full-time study rather than the piecemeal, part-time study required when all their learning must be pursued in contexts distant from their daily rounds. They also can make part-time study possible for students who otherwise could not enroll at all.

So experiential learning does seem to expand the possibilities for effective integration of professional/vocational preparation and liberal/general education. Recall some of the examples cited earlier. The Bioresearch course focused on helping students develop professional skills, research skills, and knowledge regarding bioassay techniques, and the ability to plan and carry out research projects concerning environmental problems. Experiential elements, which included encounters with polluters, films that showed stark pictures of persons and communities seriously damaged by polluted water, readings that examined the history and economics of water quality and water use, all could broaden the educational value of this study. Or take the Race Relations course. Would interviews or group meetings with persons working hard to create more equal and just conditions for minority groups—in courts, housing, education, employment—have strengthened the significance of this liberal arts study? Would it have given students a chance to see how such studies, which provide historical and cultural perspectives, contribute understandings directly pertinent to potential career alternatives?

The Counseling Theory and Practice course, which focuses primarily on professional training and related practice, asks students to reach for larger perspectives by looking at service agencies and their social contexts. Why not use some plays, poetry, novels, biographies, or films that reveal the human dimensions of obesity, learning disabilities, and consequent parent-child relationships? Would studies of other cultures—where Slenderella is no model or where valued kinds of learning are more like the strengths of the disabled than like the weaknesses prescribed by our own culture—augment their professional preparation and serve liberal arts values as well?

Early Childhood Education is unremittingly professional in its orientation, providing a broad-gauged and complex range of activities and responsibilities. Suppose that students were asked to examine films and writings that describe current patterns of child rearing and "early childhood education" in Africa, Israel, Latin America, and the Far East—or were asked to put current practices in historical perspective concerning shifting patterns in this country. Would those students see their current role and responsibilities somewhat differently? Would analyses of the strengths, weaknesses, and general value of the day care centers be improved? Would the range of innovations and improvements that occurred to them expand? I suspect so.

Consider the Human Services and Criminal Justice contract. There are some short and powerful philosophical writings concerning justice: what it means and the conditions necessary for its exercise. Attitudes toward debt and behavior toward debtors have undergone major historical transformations. Why have they occurred? What has been the role of money, banking, credit? And what are possible future consequences of these shifts? Senior citizens could be similarly considered.

Would the young man pursuing pruning and woodworking as part of his effort to become "an integral being" and maximize consciousness have found information about the lifestyles of craftsmen and about historical periods of furniture styles and cabinetmaking interesting? Would he have been intrigued by reading *The Secret Life of Plants* and reviewing some of the related research? Eastern views concerning powerful interrelations among plants, animals, and man would suggest different attitudes toward his work.

Run through the rest of the contracts. It is not difficult to add experiential elements, or to imagine materials from traditional liberal arts disciplines that would enrich professional preparation or reveal the relevance of liberal studies to a wide variety of professions or vocations.

Let us not underestimate the importance of achieving effective integration of professional/vocational preparation and liberal studies. The values are larger than improved employment and graduate school prospects for the young and increased educational effectiveness for older persons. If it is true that love and work are the basic ingredients for a meaningful existence, then we are attempting no less. For the liberal arts can expand the capacity to love life, to experience it more richly, to continually increase our range of satisfying activities. Effective professional/vocational studies, which not only prepare us for productive work but also help us grow in scope and capacity, offer the other essential. But one in the absence of the other leaves us crippled, negotiating tough terrain with difficulty, feeling less than we ought to, getting less from our lives than we know we should. Most of us share the sentiments of Robert Frost's tramp, who said:

> But yield who will to their separation
> My object in living is to unite
> My avocation and vocation
> As my two eyes make one in sight.
> For only where love and need are one
> And work is play for mortal stakes
> Then is the deed ever really done
> For heaven and the future sakes.[12]

Few of us achieve that unity; most of us strive for it. It has to be re-created continually as the life cycle and its vicissitudes toss us to and fro. A college that helps us learn how to do this makes a major contribution indeed.

The basic point is this: When we open ourselves to creative use of experiential opportunities accompanied by appropriate readings, films, and resource persons from varied disciplines, ways to integrate a professional and liberal education can be quite readily conceived. It requires no great creative leap or special talent to think of useful combinations. But academics don't do this much. I think there are two reasons for this: First, there is the bedrock problem of faculty knowledge and competence. If our education and training have led us to concentrate on one twig in a branch of knowledge attached to a tree that is a subspecialty in a particular discipline, then we are not equipped to reach across the range of possibilities even if we could imagine them. We will not think we have the necessary grasp of pertinent readings, the background to interpret and discuss general issues, the understanding required to help students make sense of diverse experiences. Often we are right. But even more often, I suspect, we could extend ourselves significantly, albeit humbly, and our students would be far better for it. Unfortunately, graduate training and the current reward systems in most colleges and universities work heavily against such adventurous efforts. They push us toward narrowly focused expertise that guarantees our hold on a small piece of professional turf. Even though it may be far out and barren, we can still call it home and stake our claim there.

Then there is the secondary effect of this pervasive orientation, which leads us to construct watertight compartments—not only between disciplines and professional studies but also between subspecialties within. Courses, curricular sequences, and requirements for certification and graduation follow suit and institutionalize fragmentation. New elements disrupt those neat patterns; trade-offs are required; time must be taken from special professional or disciplinary complexities and given over to other readings, writings, and experiences.

Many of these once watertight compartments have recently begun to leak and some are even falling apart. Interdisciplinary, problem-oriented, and thematic studies are becoming more frequent and more diverse. In many institutions formal procedures make it possible for an individual student, or a faculty member and a group of students, to create his own combinations with a minimum of red tape. The way toward more flexible integration of professional and

---

12. Robert Frost, *Two Tramps in Mudtime*.

liberal studies is opening. The growth of experiential learning is part of that increased openness and flexibility. It can help accelerate the process and add an important dimension—a sound basis for coherence and order. Listen to Dewey once again:

> It is a cardinal principle of the newer school of education that the beginning of instruction shall be made with the experience learners already have; that this experience and the capacities that have already been developed during its course provide the starting point for all further learning. I am not so sure that the other condition, that of orderly development toward expansion and organization of subject matter through growth of experience, receives as much attention. Yet the principle of continuity of education experience requires that equal thought and attention be given to...this aspect of the educational problem....
>
> It is a mistake to suppose that the principle of the leading on of experience to something different is adequately satisfied simply by giving pupils some new experiences. It is...essential that the new objects and events be related intellectually to those of earlier experiences, and this means that there be some advance made in conscious articulation of facts and ideas.... He [the educator] must constantly regard what is already won not as a fixed possession but as an agency and instrumentality for opening new fields which make new demands upon existing powers of observation and of intelligent use of memory....
>
> The problem of selection and organization of subject matter is fundamental....the basic material of study cannot be picked up in a cursory manner. Occasions which are not and cannot be foreseen are bound to arise wherever there is intellectual freedom. They should be utilized. But there is a decided difference between using them in the development of a continuing line of activity and trusting to them to provide the chief material for learning.
>
> Unless a given experience leads out into a field previously unfamiliar, no problems arise, while problems are the stimulus to thinking. That the conditions found in present experience should be used as sources of problems is a characteristic which differentiates education based upon experience from traditional education. For in the latter, problems were set from the outside. Nonetheless, growth depends upon the presence of difficulty to be overcome by the exercise of intelligence.... The new facts and new ideas thus obtained become the ground for further experiences in which new problems are presented. The process is a continuous spiral.[13]

Solutions to problems of sequence, emphasis, and timing, as well as to problems of substance and standards, are materially advanced by analyzing the requirements of experiential settings and the progressive kinds of demands that they can make. These settings give us strong and functional leverage on some of the current tendencies toward fragmentation and incoherence that have arisen in the absence of authoritatively imposed requirements. The historical requirements of traditional disciplines and professional studies are breaking down under the onslaught of new problems, new information, new insights, and of splinter professional interests. When educational activities include concrete experiences, application, and active experimentation, another basis for structure and coherence is supplied that can give order not only to particular courses or learning contracts, but to entire degree programs.

With some practice, students themselves develop the capacity to project plans that identify pertinent experiences, make use of appropriate readings and resource persons, and provide for necessary kinds of evaluation. They become competent in managing the experiential learning cycle themselves. When this happens, as it

---

13. Dewey, *Experience and Education*, pp. 74-79.

does in many cases, then the major contribution of experiential learning has been achieved. Students have "learned how to learn." They have developed an organic ability to metabolize life's steady diet of information and experience, drawing nourishment from it to replace spent energy, build new muscles, and even lay on a bit of fat against future emergencies.

When such connective links really take hold, students can move beyond recurrent education to lifelong learning. While pursuing recurrent education can be a significant step, lifelong learning is a giant stride. Recurrent education typically involves intermittent use of educational institutions and other resources for learning as particular circumstances create sufficient need; it implies a persisting separation of living and learning. Lifelong learning, however, especially when it is anchored in the experiential learning cycle, implies much more: The human creature is continually absorbed and active with his or her personal development. Experiential learning cycles flow continuously, enriching not only the individuals directly involved but also those around them through observations, reflections, abstractions, and applications. This kind of learning is not restricted to occasions of special need, recurring though such needs may be. Instead, it becomes a staff of life supporting a vigorous and healthy existence.

In this fashion we may better approximate one ideal aim of education, which is increased self-control. Impulsive reactions to the pressures or seductions of concrete experiences will still occur. But "stop and think" may be heard more clearly when there is increased skill and practice in observation, reflection, and abstract conceptualization. Thus one will be less driven by unexamined internal reactions or by unwitting acquiescence to circumstantial forces. And, conversely, increased skill and experience with active application and experimentation will help us make constructive use of authority and authoritative information without being dominated by one particular version of reality.

So the potential benefits for students and for the effectiveness and contributions of higher education may be substantial. Motives for learning may be more accurately tapped at the outset and more powerfully sustained as the challenges of varied settings and learning activities are confronted. The quality of learning may be augmented in ways that provide direct carryover into current responsibilities and interests. Retention of knowledge and information—for future application and experimentation, or as a base for further reflection and abstract conceptualization—may be improved. Opportunities are opened up for more effective integration of professional training and liberal learning which, in turn, can help students continue to achieve that integration as they encounter opportunities and setbacks. Finally, students may achieve increased control over their own impulses and reflex reactions, increased freedom from control by external authorities, and increased capacity to manage the pressures of varied settings at work, at home, and in the community. These potential benefits suggest that experiential learning deserves careful thought by any institution concerned about its educational effectiveness, whose mission is not confined either to narrowly focused professional or vocational preparation or to similarly limited liberal arts studies.

6

Potentials for Faculty and Institutions

PRESUMABLY THE POTENTIALS FOR STUDENTS AND THEIR
learning are primary considerations in decisions regarding experiential learning. But there are secondary benefits—side bets for faculty members and for the institution that can make the odds more
favorable in balancing the risks presented by the problems. These
side bets provide rewards for faculty members who invest time and
energy to develop new resources and new areas of competence,
who change their comfortable patterns of teaching for new ones
more complicated and less easy to manage. There also are rewards
for the institution that invests the additional dollars and administrative energy to get a broad-based effort under way.

One of the payoffs for faculty members is the opportunity for professional experiential learning. Faculty members can see their insights, principles, and hypothetical concepts tested against diverse
realities. The plans formulated with students and the activities they
undertake explicitly check key propositions or assumptions. As
student performances and experiences are evaluated, faculty members receive substantive feedback based not only on their own observations but on evaluative reports from field supervisors and from
the students themselves. This process, going forward as heterogen-
eous students pursue experiential learning in varied settings, provides a wealth of information on which continuous reformulations
can be used.

Although some experiential settings lend themselves to refining
special kinds of knowledge and competence, the pressures of most
settings will be toward greater breadth and greater connectedness
with other areas of inquiry and understanding. Thus the faculty
member who is interested in the ramifications of a given area of
knowledge, in its relationships to other allied or disparate areas,
will find ample opportunity to pursue those relationships with stu-

dents in the field and in preparing for future courses or contracts.

Perhaps the greatest rewards for faculty members interested in teaching will be their sense of growing potency and effectiveness and increased satisfaction in their working relationships with students, which tend to become more collegial. Greater mutuality develops in the search for new knowledge and appropriate skills. There are tasks to be done and challenges to be met, and both parties are working together. This does not diminish the importance of the faculty member's expertise and knowledge but rather increases it as the practical value of that background becomes apparent. The faculty member's resources then become more actively sought out and more thoughtfully received.

This new relationship, coupled with the fact that faculty members observe a much wider range of student performance, provides more solid information on which to rest judgments concerning educational activities and standards. When student behavior is limited to taking notes in class, participating in occasional discussions, submitting term papers, or completing examinations, only limited information is available about strengths and weaknesses, interests and aversions. But as faculty members and students proceed through those Counseling and Early Childhood Education courses, a great deal will be revealed about what each student can do well and not so well, about which each does with relish, resignation, or resistance. This information makes for more effective teaching and learning and more sound planning for future students.

Most important, perhaps, is the increased opportunity to observe real change in students as a consequence of the teaching we do and our relationships with them. When the only evidence of results are examination answers or papers, we may see brilliant performances —but we don't have much sense of the learning or change that actually has occurred. Most of us do not pretest our students at the outset so we really do not know how well they might have performed without the benefit of our wisdom. But when students enter an experiential setting that calls for active participation, contribution, observation, and analyses, we have clear evidence about their competence, insight, and knowledge at the outset. Then we get varied kinds of information about the progress they make. We can see whether their observations become more penetrating and accurate as a result of the information the course provides. We see whether they are able to modify their behavior appropriately and whether their actual performance improves. Because much of that information will be more publicly available—to field supervisors, colleagues, fellow students, and to outside evaluators if we choose to use them—our confidence in it can be better founded and more broadly based. Therefore, we can be more confident that our teaching has really made a difference.

There also can be more general benefits for the institution. Just as individual faculty members can evaluate courses and syllabi more clearly in the light of the learning that occurs for students, the implications of their experiences for theories and concepts, and the relevance of academic studies for experiential settings, so also can curriculum committees and those responsible for broader questions of institutional priority and program development have a sounder basis for judgment. This information is especially significant in various professional development areas where academic isolation and keeping the curriculum up-to-date are notorious problems. In fast-moving areas concerned with the natural, social, and behavioral sciences, significant developments can occur within a five- or ten-year period. It can often take at least that long for an institution to perceive a change, evaluate its significance, conceptualize the implications for its own program, get them through the governance system, and finally put them into action. Under these circumstances, experiential learning can provide an early warning system to signal trajectories of change coming over the horizon so that faculty can be better prepared to meet them on arrival.

There are also more immediate and practical institutional benefits. Working relationships that make available learning opportunities for students in diverse agencies, community organizations, industries, museums, and cultural enterprises dramatically expand the resources available to the institution. They become available without the capital investments, maintenance costs, and personnel expenses required if they were to be replicated on campus. These resources include not only a sharply increased range of human expertise but also facilities that can cover the full spectrum from mundane and inexpensive office space to highly specialized laboratory facilities. No institution could possibly replicate the facilities and resources used by students at institutions that have wide-ranging experiential learning activities. Without those resources, the variety of studies that could be undertaken would shrink, and the resources necessary to pursue them would expand explosively.

These expanded resources and the larger range of studies made possible in turn can broaden the enrollment base. They increase the range of students attracted to the institution and the numbers that can be well served. This is especially the case for students beyond typical college age, who cannot move into full-time residency and often must pursue part-time study. Opportunities for experiential learning that make use of settings and resources already part of their environment allow many adults to pursue higher education who otherwise could not. Others who have managed to eke out evening or weekend courses here and there can pursue higher education in a fuller, more integrated fashion.

The possibilities for strong synergy will be great when colleges recognize and grant credit for the significant experiences adults bring to education and when they learn to establish connections between education and the experiences that already are part of the love and work of adult existence. As we all recognize by now, the adult student constituency is growing rapidly and all the signs are that this growth will continue. Employers now pay for the educational activities of four million adults, and public money finances another 2.8 million. Union contracts increasingly call for educational benefits. Once these benefits become standard for large numbers and built into employment expectations, there will be no turning back. Consider the range of health and medical benefits available now in contrast to those typically provided prior to World War II. It is hard to imagine forces short of catastrophe that could turn the clock back on those changes. Educational benefits will be equally resistant to elimination.

In addition to the expanded range of resources and the broadened enrollment base, relationships between town and gown and between state and university can be substantially strengthened. When good working relationships are established with a broad range of agencies and organizations, then understanding of and support for the institution are similarly broadened and enhanced. Many persons other than faculty members, administrators, students, and alumni come to have an investment in its continued welfare and survival. Incidents or accidents of a few students, deviance or indiscretions of an occasional faculty member or administrator, can create a highly distorted image. When there has been widespread experience of students, faculty, and administrators through functional relationships, then those inevitable occasions are seen in perspective.

Community support and understanding can become especially strong as increased numbers of adults enroll and use institutional resources to serve their interests in professional advancement, community service, leisure activities, and improved family relationships. Often these adult students will be in positions of corporate or community leadership. Their influence with legislators and potential donors can be a substantial cut above that of younger alumni. They have firsthand and up-to-date information about the institution and can speak persuasively out of their own direct experiences. If experiential learning lives up to some of its potential for improving educational effectiveness, then the assertions of adult students will not only have greater validity than in the past but the evidence for those claims will be more apparent in the success such students have achieved and the kinds of persons they have become.

7

Costs

THE PROBLEMS AND POTENTIALS OF EXPERIENTIAL LEARN-
ing have been examined in some detail. Unfortunately, hard data
that clearly isolate the cost benefits of experiential learning relative
to other educational approaches are not available. Thus we have no
objectively established benchmarks against which cost differentials
might be considered. There is, however, a wealth of more general
research concerning college impacts and human development that
suggests that institutional changes toward experiential learning will
result in increased educational effectiveness. (See, for example,
A.W. Astin and R.J. Panos, *The Educational and Vocational Development of College Students*; A.W. Chickering, *Education and Iden-
tity*; K.A. Feldman and T.M. Newcomb, *The Impact of College on
Students*; L. Murphy and E. Raushenbush, *Achievement in the College Years*; T.M. Newcomb, K. Koenig, R. Flacks, and D.P. Warwick,
*Persistence and Change: A College and Its Students After Twenty-
Five Years*; E. Raushenbush, *The Student and His Studies*; N. San-
ford, *Self and Society: Social Change and Individual Development*;
R.W. White, *Lives in Progress: A Study of the Natural Growth of
Personality*.) This is not the place to review the basic findings from
this literature; we will have to let research evidence of benefits rest
with that general assertion. Any institution will be helped to assess
potential benefits by a good grasp of this work.

Getting a clear picture of relative costs is not easy. First, we need
to recognize that there are three parties to this particular cost picture: the educational institution, the cooperating agency, and the
student. All three cost elements must be taken into account. What
are the agency costs in staff time, space, facilities, equipment, and
supplies? What are the added student costs in travel expenses,
clothes, special equipment or supplies? Most agencies and students
could make rough estimates, and we ought to have such information;

but so far I have not been able to discover any. The primary interest for most readers will be the costs for a single educational institution. Sound data are not readily available here, either, but we can suggest some things to consider that will help a college or university make intelligent guesses.

Some basic principles: First, like any other enterprise, colleges and universities are subject to forces of supply and demand. Their financial condition is a function of the costs they incur in providing education and other services in relation to the demand for what they offer. A programmatic alternative that increases demand may generate income that more than offsets added costs. In addition, it may create a broader and more stable financial base. When budgetary pressures hit, we often spend more time figuring out how to reduce costs than trying to find ways to increase demand. We step up recruiting activities and sometimes consider new areas of content to meet a fad or an emerging interest. But we seldom consider changes in structure, location, educational processes, or resources that might make our institution accessible to new constituencies.

It also is useful to distinguish between efficiency and effectiveness. Efficiency increases when either quality or quantity improves faster than costs, or when costs remain constant. Effectiveness increases when results improve regardless of costs. Efficiency, therefore, can be viewed as a function of relationships between effectiveness and costs. Efficiency and effectiveness can vary somewhat independently. An hour-long videotaped lecture to 10,000 students in mutiple locations might be highly efficient but much less effective than if the same material were covered with groups of 15 in two-hour seminars. What we all are striving for is to maximize efficiency and effectiveness at the same time. For an excellent discussion of these issues, see *Colleges and Money*, Chapter 3, "Facts and Fictions About Educational Efficiency " (Change Magazine Press).

Applying these principles to experiential learning gives us the following questions: Will the demand for services increase if we change in this direction, and if so, how much? Will the increased demand and income thereby generated offset added costs? Will the relationships between the efficiency of experiential learning programs and their educational effectiveness exceed or fall short of the alternatives currently provided? All of these questions require estimates concerning two sets of costs. One set—the dollars required for added staff, space, equipment, supplies, and travel—is relatively easy to estimate and control. The other set—the consequences for other institutional costs—is more difficult to ascertain and influence.

Only a few words need to be said about the first set. Each institution will arrive at its own expenditure levels in ways consistent with past practices. A good beginning can be made with a full-time director supported by a full-time secretary who is mature and competent enough to handle certain kinds of calls, contacts, and correspondence independently, and who can help keep a complex operation well organized and running smoothly. Travel money will vary significantly with location. An urban context with inexpensive public transportation will require very little; a rural context where experiential learning settings may span a 30- to 50-mile radius will require much more. In rural conditions it also may be necessary to provide some transportation assistance for students. Telephone costs also can vary substantially with location. The main area in which to spend money at the outset is in obtaining the most highly qualified and respected person possible as director. Skimp there and not only future costs but potential income are apt to be very low indeed, because the program will not go anywhere.

We can make a start in considering the other set of costs by posing questions concerning elements of current operations likely to be influenced by new experiential learning programs:

1. *Will admission and recruitment processes become more efficient or less? If we develop systematic relationships with varied businesses, human service agencies, and cultural organizations, will they become steady sources of students who need to meet recurrent educational needs? Will new alternatives—that make it more possible for older students to integrate work, family, and community responsibilities with their educational programs—increase the number of adults who want to enroll? If so, will dealing with their inquiries require more or less time and effort? Will we need new forms, new criteria, and new admissions processes to serve them? Will recruitment activities to reach these potential new constituencies be more complicated and time consuming than our customary round of college nights and high school visits? Will more students stay with us longer and return more frequently? Will the frequency of dropping in and dropping out, together with the added costs of processing those changes, increase? Or will students tend to continue in more regular fashion?*

2. *Will the kinds of students attracted to our experiential learning alternatives need more or less financial aid than those currently enrolled? Will the potential wages and stipends available in some experiential settings reduce need? Or will the added expenses of utilizing those settings increase it?*

3. *Will demand for educational advising, career planning, and personal counseling increase or drop? Will more time, energy, and competence be required from faculty, student personnel professionals, and counselors?*

4. *Will it be possible to increase the student-faculty ratio for experiential learning programs because of the teaching and evaluation of field supervisors? Or will the faculty time required for developing and maintaining those working relationships call for fewer rather than more students?*

5. *Will the per-student costs of educational facilities and resources rise or drop? Will it be necessary to increase the range of our library holdings, or will on-site reading materials reduce the need for on-campus collections? Will specialized laboratory facilities and experiences elsewhere mean that our own facilities can be reserved for basic uses? Or will the special questions and problems encountered in the field increase the demand for unique equipment and materials that may have only limited use?*

6. *Will experiential learning reduce pressures on classroom space so that greater scheduling flexibility is possible and larger numbers of students can be accommodated? Or will there be increased need for small group discussions, seminars, workshops, and informal meetings so that current pressures will grow rather than drop?*

7. *Will off-campus experiential learning encourage students to*

move out of college residences into their own apartments or cooper-
atives? Will there be pressure for residency periods of varying
lengths, flexibly managed throughout the year, to alternate with experiential learning requirements and opportunities? If so, will the
amounts or periods of occupancy be greater or less? Will the costs
of assigning and keeping track of residents increase?

8. How much will administrative costs increase? We can calculate the costs of a new position and office, but what will the added
time invested by other administrators cost? What will their added
travel expenses amount to? How much extra work will be generated
for their secretaries?

These clusters of questions and some of the earlier observations
can be converted into the following general guidelines for estimating
costs and for collecting the information necessary to do so:

1. Identify the numbers and kinds of new students likely to enroll
and project potential income.

2. Project personnel costs for a director and secretary, supplies
and expense money needed, and travel funds required—including
those for students, if necessary.

3. Estimate added costs or savings in recruitment, admissions processes, and materials.

4. Estimate increases or decreases in financial aid requests. Estimate wages and stipends available from various experiential learning settings. Estimate potential sources of support from unions, businesses, social agencies, and the like.

5. Estimate costs for additional staff, time, and scheduling
changes to provide educational advising and personal counseling.

6. Specify anticipated student-faculty ratios. If they are higher or
lower than ratios for current alternatives, estimate the differences
in savings or costs.

7. Estimate consequences for space utilization including labora-
tories, seminar rooms, and lounges for small group meetings as well
as classrooms.

8. Estimate consequences for residential facilities and food
services and calculate differences in income and expenses.

9. Estimate costs associated with extra time, travel, and secretarial services for administrators other than the director.

I wish we could share answers to the questions or solid information from diverse types of institutions that could inform your
estimates in these varied areas. Unfortunately, I know of no such
information currently available. There may well be in-house documents prepared by a particular college or university as part of its
own planning and development that would be helpful, but they are
not in the public realm.

A collection of individual cases would be extremely helpful to
others who need to make educated guesses about costs and savings
in their particular circumstances. A project that collected such information from a diverse set of experienced institutions and then
developed some general guidelines would be most valuable at this
juncture. It could provide a set of concrete institutional experiences
on which other institutions might reflect. It could lay the foundation
for general concepts and hypotheses that might be the object of
active experimentation by institutions interested in moving in the
direction of experiential learning. Without such systematic informa-

tion, each of us will have to generalize from other budgetary experiences with our institution, consult with those from similar institutions who have more experience, and predict shifting costs, recognizing that our error in either direction may be substantial.

8

Policy Implications

THROUGHOUT THIS VOLUME, WE HAVE FOCUSED ON EXPER-
iential learning at the institutional level, on the kinds of changes,
problems, potentials, and costs involved if a college or university is
to move toward more substantial integration of concrete experiences and active applications with reflection and abstract conceptualization. These institutional changes will be encouraged or
hampered by policies and practices of various national, regional,
and state organizations. In closing, it may be useful to identify some
key areas that need attention if sound use of experiential learning is
to be encouraged.

At the outset, we need to recognize that current moves toward
experiential learning are part of a broad-based effort to improve
access and equity in higher education. These efforts have a long history, but they accelerated sharply during the 1960s. Despite setbacks here and there in response to budgetary pressures, such efforts are still under way, finding expression in basic modifications
of admissions practices, curricular content, learning processes,
graduation requirements, institutional purposes, and staffing and
organizational structures. Experiential learning draws strength
from and contributes to this major movement throughout higher
education.

There is still much to be done. As Morris Keeton points out, "It
would be a gross mistake to imagine that we have made an end even
of identifying these sources of inequity and inefficiency.... Among
the worst of our sins has been the acceptance of existing limitations
as to who should have access to education, what the range of legitimate learning options should be, what degree of respect should be
given to different kinds of learning and learners, and how institutions of postsecondary education should be organized and coordinated. These limitations have, in turn, rested upon limits within our

vision of the best available strategies for instruction and learning and of the ways in which the learning that has occurred can be identified and reported."[14]

Because experiential learning makes use of, helps foster, and gives credit for diverse abilities beyond verbal skills and academic competence, it opens opportunities for successful performance and learning to a wide range of students whose major strengths lie outside the priorities set by an exclusively bookish orientation. We have reached the point where many colleges and universities are willing to open their enrollment to blue-collar workers, minority group members, housewives, and the elderly. Experiential learning can help open interior doors to achievement and growth once these new students cross the threshold. Thus it responds to national policies and principles concerning equal opportunity.

Unfortunately, however, the policies and practices of some national agencies run directly counter to the contributions experiential learning can make. The most blatant example is a 1977 ruling by the Veterans Administration that links financial support to class attendance. Certainly there were abuses that needed attention; and there is much experiential learning built into regular courses and classes carried on in traditional fashion. But there are many educationally sound and powerful uses of experiential learning, fully sanctioned by college faculties and appropriate professionals, that are either excluded or seriously hampered by the VA guidelines. Some institutions have coped by using verbal gymnastics. At others, educational alternatives for veterans have had to be restricted or bent out of shape. At still others, enrollment of veterans has fallen off sharply.

Perhaps a more significant though less blatant problem is the pervasive bias against financial aid for part-time students. Although experiential learning can incorporate ongoing experiences and responsibilities and thus permit larger numbers of students to enroll full time, certain arrangements are well suited to large numbers of students who must remain employed and who therefore must study part time and who have financial need. Yet most financial aid policies are oriented toward full-time students. Even where program policies permit support for part-time students or for off-campus activities, as with federal student grants, not many actually receive aid. The attitude of financial aid officers remains one of the greatest obstacles. They often see part-time students in experiential programs as "nontraditional" and a nuisance.

But the hurdles are still more complex. The first problem for the part-time student is to obtain the necessary information and forms. The distribution systems are designed to reach high school seniors or students already enrolled in college. Little is done to inform students outside those contexts about the kinds of financial assistance available. Nothing is done to help them cope with the numerous forms required. High school and college students can obtain assistance from counselors and financial aid officers. Those who are on campus infrequently or who are there outside the usual 9-to-5 working day have difficulty getting help.

Obtaining the necessary information and forms, however, only puts the student in a position to deal with more fundamental prob-

---

14. M. Keeton, "Credentials for the Learning Society," in Keeton, *Experiential Learning*, p. 2.

lems. The formulas used for eligibility are designed basically for young, "dependent" students. Even when they recognize the "independent" student, they seem to assume a young adult who has a high percentage of disposable effective income available for educational purposes. The middle- or low-income person with dependents is discriminated against. Program guidelines themselves often discriminate when they are designed to offer "four years of assistance to recent high school graduates." Such guidelines obviously do not encourage adult or part-time students, although legally such persons may not be barred from receiving aid. Work-study programs are another source of financial aid. But they, too, are designed for students without major responsibilities. Persons employed full time or half time, or who have substantial family obligations, find it virtually impossible to participate. Yet, large sums of financial aid are allocated to such programs.[15]

Married women experience further difficulties; usually the husband's support is required. Unless a wife has an independent income that is not crucial to her family's support, her husband must share his income or be willing to sign for a loan. He must participate in the complex processes of applying for aid and thereby admit to an implication of inadequacy as a "provider." A variety of federal, state, and private funders make financial aid available for a married woman without her husband's signature only when family income falls below the subsistence level. Clearly, the whole system of financing postsecondary education for part-time students calls for a major overhaul. Until substantial progress is made in that area, equity and access will be limited—and the potential contributions of experiential learning to this major movement in higher education will be similarly constrained.

Experiential learning not only assumes that there are many kinds of useful learning but also that there are many ways to learn and many places where learning can occur. As those assumptions become more widely held, the need for a new kind of regional institution is becoming apparent—an institution that can help students identify those opportunities for learning best suited to their individual purposes, backgrounds, and current realities. Such an institution may offer not only advice and counsel concerning appropriate institutions, programs, or combinations thereof but also assessment services so that students can determine the competence and knowledge they currently have in terms of their purposes and in terms of varied entrance requirements or credentials. Current institutional forms vary from heavy emphasis on evaluation and credentialing with limited counseling, exemplified by the New York State Regents External Degree Program, to heavy emphasis on counseling with limited evaluation, exemplified by the National Center for Educational Brokering.[16] Experiential learning fuels the need for a national network of such institutions, supported publicly as an integral part of the postsecondary education system. Without such a network, students who recognize the value of experiential learning and who need to put together effective combinations to meet their own

15. This information concerning financial aid for part-time students comes from information supplied by John Hall, dean of student services at Empire State College.
16. For further information, write to: Regents External Degree Program, The University of the State of New York, 99 Washington Avenue, Albany, N.Y. 12210; and National Center for Educational Brokering, 405 Oak Street, Syracuse, N.Y. 13203.

purposes must operate on a hit-or-miss basis, relying upon the limited information they pick up from friends, advertising, news releases, and the importunings of recruiting institutions. Our experiences with experimental models have been sufficient to get out most of the major bugs. Now it is time to move on.

The rising expectations concerning the range of legitimate college-level learning and appropriate locations and resources are adding pressures for the reform of degree definitions. These pressures are felt at both the national and state levels. The Higher Education General Information Survey (HEGIS) reporting codes provide a good example of a historic relic that needs updating. The degree program descriptors are limited almost entirely to traditional disciplinary and professional categories. Certainly, most students' majors will fit quite comfortably into those boxes for some time to come—but additional categories are needed to recognize diverse individual and programmatic alternatives that have flourished during the past 10 years.

To be sure, the general interdisciplinary categories can serve as copious wastebaskets, but they often are inappropriate. The root problem is that many major programs are not basically disciplinary, interdisciplinary, or professional. Many programs are geared to some social problem: population control, nuclear energy, pollution, resource management, race relations, world peace, the politics of food, and so on. Other programs are oriented to various area studies and thematic concentrations concerning ethnic or minority groups, the role of women, and the like. You can crowd these programs under various interdisciplinary umbrellas because they do make use of information, principles, and research methods drawn from diverse sources. It is somewhat helpful to have the interdisciplinary loopholes. Institutions trying to get new alternatives under way would like to be conscientious in their reporting. Furthermore, they would like positive support from a national framework that recognizes emerging needs and institutional responses to them. In addition, as the ratio of misinformation begins to outrun accurate representation, HEGIS purposes are increasingly ill-served and the decisions based on HEGIS data become more and more inaccurate. The time has come for some major improvements.

The effects of the HEGIS codes become even more significant when they are adopted by states as categories for program registration. Then all new majors or degree programs have to fit these limited descriptors. Any institution trying to develop new alternatives that respond to increasingly diverse educational constituencies and their varied needs finds itself tightly constrained. It may be creative enough to crowd complex and sometimes unruly collections into a few small lifeboats, but it then becomes necessary to keep a weather eye on the horizon lest a squall from the state education department strike unexpectedly. You can hear the comments clearly: "Perhaps a degree program that emphasizes alternate technological systems for low-cost, low-energy housing can be justified under the environmental studies rubric. But tell us, please, just where did you classify this major in the Ecology of Integral Being, with its work in tree pruning and woodworking? Religion, you say? Isn't that quite a leap of faith?"

One wants to be ready. The point is not that such a study should be prohibited or that such a descriptor should be censored. It is probably an apt and accurate description of what that student really was all about. At least it deserves hard-nosed examination of the substance, methods of evaluation, evidence, and criteria used. It may be extremely valuable, or both student and faculty member may be caught in a *folie à deux*, kidding themselves about the great things that are happening. Of course, such self-deceptions are not entirely unknown in traditional courses and majors either.

The problem with the HEGIS codes and their use by state education departments and others is that students and faculty members are not encouraged to develop new programs when they are appropriate. If they do have the courage to do so, there is a great temptation to adopt a rhetoric and an overlay of clearly respectable titles and activities. This camouflage lets the important activities go on without being blown out of the water. The unfortunate thing about this response is that some valuable innovative programs are neither shared with others who might profit from them nor subjected to open and rational criticism that could lead to more effectiveness.

The consequences are even more dysfunctional when a conspiracy of silence develops between the faculty members and students who venture into new areas and the administrators or senior faculty members responsible for monitoring educational substance and quality. Then a kind of in-house language and private signal system develops with which the faculty member says: "I'm getting into these areas; but don't worry, I'll keep it cool." The senior person responds: "Okay, but don't push it too far. We're not prepared to surface these issues just yet." That dynamic has an insidious effect on faculty morale, educational effectiveness, and institutional progress. It casts a pall over experiential efforts and serves neither the students, the college, nor the state.

At the state level there is another problematic aspect to the degree definition problem. It is best exemplified by the way requirements for Bachelor of Arts (BA), Bachelor of Science (BS), and Bachelor of Professional Studies (BPS) degrees are customarily defined. In New York State, for example, the distinctions are simple to state and easy to remember: The BA degree must be at least 75 percent liberal arts and no more than 25 percent professional studies; the BS may be up to 50 percent professional studies; and the BPS may be up to 75 percent professional studies. But these simple definitions are not so easy to apply. The first problem is that the meaning and boundaries of the liberal arts have become increasingly imponderable. The growing abstractions produced by various faculty task forces do not provide very sure guides for particular courses or activities. And the operational definitions that formerly rested in the traditional disciplines have become increasingly open to question.

The second problem is that many professions require complex knowledge and competence that looks much like some long-standing liberal arts disciplines; when we observe students tackling professional experiences and reading pertinent literature thoughtfully and critically, we see effects very much like our liberal arts outcomes. Recall the course on Counseling Theory and Practice, for example. Much of that course qualifies as professional preparation. But what of those elements that examine relationships between counseling and human services and the social contexts in which they are rendered? When students read *Asylums, Schools Without Failure, The Myth of Mental Illness,* and similar works, when they examine the actual practices of social agencies and the attitudes toward health, illness, human dignity, and social welfare embedded in them, are they not developing the critical capacity, observational skill, breadth of knowledge, complexity of insight, and cultural understanding necessary for effective citizenship and social awareness? Or consider the contract in the course on Human Services and Criminal Justice, which is part of a degree program to prepare for graduate school in social work and to obtain direct practice in that profession. What do we call it when the student studies the American prison system from sociological, psychological, economic, and political viewpoints?

The basic point is that many institutions need to create courses, contracts, programmatic alternatives, and majors that effectively integrate professional/vocational training with liberal and general education. We have degree definitions that require us to break those components apart and compute percentages of each. Of course, that exercise can only be carried out in crude fashion, and most authorities are too sophisticated to challenge anything but flagrant abuses. So the direct effects of such definitions are seldom felt. But like the HEGIS codes, the indirect effects can be unfortunate. The energy spent coping with such anachronisms could better be used in dealing with the serious substantive problems that must be met to develop sound alternatives for emerging needs. What we need from public authorities is strong encouragement and help, not soft and slippery imposition of outmoded requirements. The growing use of experiential learning will exacerbate this problem. To realize the potential of this new development and to guard against its problematic elements, we need far more understanding, competence, and practical skill than we now have. It is hard to carry on any work well when one arm is busy fending off reluctant dragons.

Finally, experiential learning has raised basic questions for those arbiters of educational quality and institutional status, the regional accrediting associations. Generally speaking, they have made a concerted effort to tackle the tough problems posed by the rapidly growing use of experiential learning and by the escalation of innovative alternatives during the 1970s. They have tried to do so in ways that encourage rather than stifle, that recognize sound efforts and hold up those that seem less so. Many people are exercising extremely helpful leadership, but there also are some dragging anchors. Standards and practices vary significantly from region to region. Despite the early efforts of the Federation of Regional Accrediting Commissions in Higher Education (FRACHE) and its task forces, and despite the recent development of the Council on Post-Secondary Accreditation (COPA), it is a moot point whether or not the tide has turned toward greater national consistency. The problem of national consistency for the accrediting associations is especially severe because differences among these bodies tend to reflect underlying regional differences in receptivity to experiential learning and to educational innovation. When the state systems, dominant institutions, and persons in leadership positions do not see eye to eye, then it is difficult to create reasonably common accreditation standards and equitable action.

Significant though they may be, however, these implications for financial aid, brokering and evaluation, and reporting and approval frameworks are only whitecaps on a larger ground swell of social change and needed responses by higher education, of which experiential learning is itself a part. Robert Kirkwood has put the fundamental issues unequivocably before us:

> A major problem with the traditional academic system for experiential learning...is its pretensions to the divinity of the commandments without any evidence of the revelation.... Creating an accepted system of credit for experiential learning under these conditions, therefore, will require more than effort and imagination: It will require examining the assumptions underlying all practices involved in granting educational credit, whether for classroom or off-campus learning. Indeed, we need to achieve a new basis for assessing all learning rather than to create separate procedures and standards for crediting experiential learning.
>
> The issue of crediting such learning is thus timely and directly in line with other challenges confronting higher education. To the extent that we welcome it as an opportunity to relate it to changing concepts of what constitutes legitimate learning and the characteristics of an educated person, to that extent we will further the idea of education as a continuum, embracing rather than excluding the vast potentialities for human development. With proper attention to the assessment of this learning, there need be no dilution or demeaning of the symbols we have traditionally bestowed for educational achievement....
>
> It is the integrity of the process whereby we determine the value and validity of all learning, not only of experiential learning, that will influence the credibility and public acceptance of postsecondary education. We must find improved means for communicating the essence of our endeavors, and the evidence must be substantial. Unless we honestly try, we shall find increasingly troublesome the task of convincing students and parents and legislators that the educational community deserves their support. Such support will no longer be forthcoming simply on the basis of faith or tradition.
>
> As educators, then, we have a professional responsibility to define and establish measures that are clear, equitable, and relevant to the objectives of the course, curriculum, institution, or framework in which we expect or intend to have learning take place. Few aspects of postsecondary education are in greater need of thoughtful and creative endeavor than the means and methods of assessing results. And I can see no reason why our efforts should be confined to the area of experiential learning. They should apply universally to every facet of teaching and learning. In short, the issues raised in consideration of credit for experiential learning go to the heart of the current crisis of confidence in the academic enterprise.[17]

Whether or not we agree with Kirkwood that there is a "current crisis of confidence," there is no question that issues raised by experiential learning go to the heart of the academic enterprise. Experiential learning leads us to question the assumptions and conventions underlying many of our practices. It turns us away from credit hours and calendar time toward competence, working knowledge, and information pertinent to jobs, family relationships, community responsibilities, and broad social concerns. It reminds us that higher education can do more than develop verbal skills and deposit information in those storage banks between the ears. It can contribute to more complex kinds of intellectual development and to more pervasive dimensions of human development required for effective citizenship. It can help students cope with shifting develop-

---

17. R. Kirkwood, "Importance of Assessing Learning," in Keeton, *Experiential Learning*, pp. 151-155.

mental tasks imposed by the life cycle and rapid social change.

If these potentials are to be realized, major changes in the current structures, processes, and content of higher education will be required. The campus will no longer be the sole location for learning, the professor no longer the sole source of wisdom. Instead, campus facilities and professorial expertise will be resources linked to a wide range of educational settings, to practitioners, field supervisors, and adjunct faculty. This linking together will be achieved through systematic relationships with cultural organizations, businesses, social agencies, museums, and political and governmental operations. We no longer will bind ourselves completely to the procrustean beds of fixed time units set by semester, trimester, or quarter systems, which stretch some learning to the point of transparency and lop off other learning at the head or foot. Instead, such systems will be supplemented by flexible scheduling options that tailor time to the requirements for learning and to the working realities of various experiential opportunities. Educational standards and credentials will increasingly rest on demonstrated levels of knowledge and competence as well as on actual gains made by students and the value added by college programs. We will recognize the key significance of differences among students not only in verbal skills and academic preparation but also in learning styles, capacity for independent work, self-understanding, social awareness, and human values. Batch processing of large groups will be supplemented by personalized instruction and contract learning.

The academy and the professoriat will continue to carry major responsibility for research activities, for generating new knowledge, and for supplying the perspectives necessary to cope with the major social problems rushing toward us. That work will be enriched and strengthened by more broad-based faculty and student participation and by its wide-ranging links to ongoing experiential settings.

Who can say whether these utopian prophecies will come true? Perhaps the issues raised by experiential learning will be addressed by only a small number of institutions where local pressures or purposes create propitious conditions. Their efforts may sufficiently satisfy student demand, funds, and interest so that the rest of the system continues undisturbed. We may end up with two contrasting systems harnessed uneasily together, like an ox and a stallion, trying to drag higher education forward on the rocky road and in the rough weather ahead. That alternative would be better than none. But a more promising future lies ahead if the issues raised by experiential learning are addressed widely throughout higher education, avoiding the compartmentalization of disparate camps, pulling together with well-coordinated steps and a steady pace.

Suggested Readings

Astin, A.W., *et al. Faculty Development in a Time of Retrenchment*. New Rochelle, N.Y.: Change Magazine Press, 1974.

This short but comprehensive booklet provides a set of fundamental recommendations for the professional development of faculty members. The activities recommended set a solid foundation for the kinds of changes necessary for increased competence concerning experiential learning.

Breen, P., Donlon, T. and Whitaker, U. *The Learning and Assessment of Interpersonal Skills: Guidelines for Administrators and Faculty*, CAEL Working Paper No. 4. Princeton, N.J.: Educational Testing Service, 1975.

A first attempt to tackle the complex area of interpersonal competence, this working paper offers a definition of interpersonal literacy as a basic conceptual framework. It amplifies Sidney Fine's "people skills" from the *Dictionary of Occupational Titles* to provide some helpful guidelines for those venturesome enough to recognize this fundamental area of human competence and knowledge.

Dewey, J. *Experience and Education*. New York: Collier Books, 1963.

Dewey wrote this pocket-size, 91-page volume in response to both the excesses and the criticisms of progressive education. Its balanced and practical view, rooted in sound psychology concerning teaching and learning, makes it one of the best statements available about conditions and practices that maximize teaching effectiveness.

Duley, J.S. and Gordon, Sheila. *College-Sponsored Experiential Learning: A CAEL Handbook*. Princeton, N.J.: Cooperative Assessment of Experiential Learning, 1977.

Written by professionals experienced in both two- and four-year colleges, this how-to-do-it handbook tells you everything you need to know about developing and administering experiential learning activities. Most experienced professionals will find new material in it. Those new to the task will find it clear, easy to use, and very helpful.

Keeton, Morris T. and Associates. *Experiential Learning: Rationale, Characteristics, and Assessment*. San Francisco: Jossey-Bass, 1976.

A major product of the CAEL Project, this volume addresses broad educational issues as well as practical considerations. The chapters for experiential learning prior to enrollment are the best available.

Kolb, D. and Fry, R. "Toward an Applied Theory of Experiential Learning." In *Theories of Group Processes*, edited by Cary Cooper. London/New York: John Wiley and Sons, 1975.

This paper posits an experiential learning cycle and describes results for students in various disciplines and professions who completed Kolb's "Learning Style Inventory." Implications for education and career planning are discussed.

Meyer, P. *Awarding College Credit for Non-college Learning: A Guide to Current Practices*. San Francisco: Jossey-Bass, 1975.

The focus here is entirely on crediting learning from experiences prior to college. It is a thorough and sound treatment, reasonably up-to-date in a fast-moving area.

Sexton, R.F. and Ungerer, R.A. *Rationales for Experiential Education*, ERIC Higher Education Research Report No. 3. Washington, D.C.: U.S. Government Printing Office, 1975.

This report surveys a broad range of literature concerning experiential education. Three general sections explore concepts relating to individual learning, new conditions in the world of work, and the role of the student as participant in social and political processes. It closes with a comprehensive bibliography.

Stephenson, J.B. and Sexton, R.F. "Experiential Education and the Revitalization of the Liberal Arts." In *The Philosophy of the Curriculum: The Need for General Education*, edited by Sidney Hook, Paul Kurtz, and Miro Todorovich. Buffalo, N.Y.: Prometheus Books, 1971.

This chapter presents a well-articulated dicussion of the contributions of experiential education to major liberal arts values. It suggests ways in which experiential learning contributes to issues of value, purpose, historical perspective, social responsibility, and self-awareness.

Tatzell, M. *Prospects and Methods for Interpersonal Studies*, CAEL Special Project Report. Princeton, N.J.: Educational Testing Service, 1977.

This report deals with practical considerations involved in developing and evaluating learning activities designed to foster increased interpersonal competence. It suggests several basic principles and provides concrete illustrations drawn from Empire State College learning contracts.

Tatzell, M. and Lamdin, L. *Interpersonal Learning in an Academic Setting: Theory and Practice*, CAEL Special Report. Princeton, N.J.: Educational Testing Service, 1976.

This paper treats the place of interpersonal competence in the college curriculum more generally than the Tatzell paper above. It suggests how studies designed to foster interpersonal competence meet the needs of several types of students and serve diverse educational purposes.

Torbert, W.R. *Learning From Experience Toward Consciousness*. New York/London: Columbia University Press, 1972.

"Inquiry in action can lead to learning from experience." Torbert examines in detail processes that underlie this proposition, describes varied approaches to experiential learning, and discusses problems of measuring outcomes.

FOUR OTHER IMPORTANT FACULTY POLICY PAPERS

Order from Change Magazine Press,
NBW Tower, New Rochelle, NY 10801

Faculty Development in a Time of Retrenchment. This report presents fifteen significant recommendatons for those who want to achieve continuing human, intellectual and professional growth in the challenging academic environment of the '70s. $2.95* each; $1.95 each for 10 or more copies.

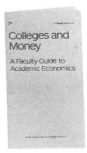

Colleges and Money. A national panel of prominent academic management and economic authorities sums up what everyone should know about the economics of education. $2.95* each; $2.50 each for 10 or more copies.

The Testing and Grading of Students. A fresh approach to the crucial issues of classroom testing and student evaluation. Evaluation of academic performance has become a subject of increasing contention among college students, and this new publication promises to shed light on a controversial subject. $2.95* each; $2.50 each for 10 or more copies.

Professional Development: A Guide to Resources. A comprehensive resource book for faculty in search of the best reference material available on teaching resources, learning and students, course development, curriculum, advising, faculty development, administrative development, faculty evaluation, and institutional change. $3.95* each; $3.00 each for 10 or more copies.

*Please note that there is a $1.00 charge for billed orders for books.

Notes on Learning Contracts

Notes on Learning Contracts

Notes on Learning Contracts

Notes on Learning Contracts

Notes on Learning Contracts

F--

M*